FUNdamental Fitness®

PLAYGROUND EXERCISES FOR GROWNUPS

BY JEN HOEFT

First Edition
First Printing
December 2004

© 2004 by Jen Hoeft

Library of Congress Control Number: 2004098666
ISBN: 0-9762868-0-7

READ PUBLISHING
3918 DORCAS DRIVE
NASHVILLE, TN 37215
615-383-1112

COVER PHOTO: Shannon Fontaine
COVER AND BOOK DESIGN: Diana Springfield & Beth Kindig
PHOTOS OF EXERCISES: Shannon Fontaine
PHOTOS OF CHILDREN: Shannon Fontaine and Jen Hoeft

DISCLAIMER

None of the techniques presented in this book are intended to treat or prevent any physical, medical, or mental condition. You should always consult a qualified health care professional before beginning any exercise program. The authors, publishers and retailers of this material specifically disclaim any and all responsibility for any injury or condition which may arise from the execution of these exercises or related activities.

CONTENTS

ACKNOWLEDGMENTS

A lot of this book is Dan DeFigio's Five Movement language and functional fitness concepts. He is a marvelous teacher and friend, and I am forever grateful.
Thanks to Bill Nagel for being a forerunner in this industry. His research and foresight are essential to the energy of this book!
Thank you Diana Springfield for calmly and patiently preparing and repairing my manuscript...and a big thank you to Beth Kindig for beautifully polishing it for me!
Shannon Fontaine, you have a magnificent eye, and a huge heart!
Thank you for the photos (see www.shannonfontaine.com, for all of his work).
Dan Bodanis, thank you for advising and coaching me the whole way through the process.
Thanks to my family and friends who constantly cheered me on...
with a special thank you to Michael, for dreaming up this project with me.
My clients get a lot of credit for letting me "experiment" with them....
And a huge thank you to the children...without you, this would have been impossible!
In order of appearance...Rachel, Claire, Taylor, Dauz, Lindsey, Joey, Lindsay, Anna, Jay, Jesus, Cheyanna, Rayna, Roan, Kaila, Allyson, Emily, Seth, Daniel, Jesse, Justice, Adam, and Ainsley.

A special thank you to you, the reader, for being open, adventurous, and ready to make a change. Welcome!

*For comments, to purchase exercise equipment, or
for more information about feeling good, eating well, and supplementing your diet,
visit* **www.jenhoeft.com**

FOREWORD

Since 1993, I have had the distinct pleasure of working with Jen Hoeft. I was fortunate to have this innovative, insightful and bright fitness professional join my powerhouse team of trainers. It was the best move I could have made.

Having been blessed to work so closely with Jen over the years, we have harnessed her positive physical and spiritual energy and developed a simple and effective system of exercise, which focuses on **fundamental types of movements** rather than specific muscles. Muscles don't work in isolation, they work in systems and groups, and in order to have a functional workout, you must train your body with this in mind. If you spend your valuable exercise time with gizmos that promise to "work your lower abs," not only are you getting ripped off, you are wasting your time. In order to create a fully functional, high-performance body, training with *The Five Movements* is a must.

As I travel the country presenting educational workshops for fitness professionals, I am encouraged to see that the national trend of fitness is moving toward functionality and practicality. The system of *FUNdamental Fitness* presented in this book is the perfect summary of this concept, geared toward creating a personalized, fun, and fully functional workout that can be done anywhere.

Enjoy, and don't forget to have fun!

Dan DeFigio
Director, Basics and Beyond[SM]
www.gettingfit.com

PART ONE
THE
INTRODUCTION

Do you remember playing "kick the can" from just after dinner until long after dark? Can you think back to a time when you sat cross-legged on the floor and played cards for hours? Did you jump rope? Stand on your head? Do the splits? Play ball? Ride your bike? Do you remember when you didn't feel tired? When you hated to go to bed?

Adults have forgotten how to feel good! The last time that most of us felt great, we were kids...we ate consistently, and nutritionally, we had less stress, play was our job, and our metabolism was *kickin'!* I wanted this ease and joy back! I wanted to feel inspired when I woke up, I wanted to like my body...I wanted to *like my life.*

I began the journey towards balance, physically. As I reminded my body how to move, play, laugh, and jump, I was able to access other areas of my life that needed balancing. *FUNdamental Fitness*, is about finding a physical trigger to jumpstart your metabolism, your memory, and your desire for feeling good. These movements are a melting pot of styles that mimic the motions of our childhood. Let the concept sink in and act as a catalyst for *your own* ideas of balance, joy, health and *FUN!*

FUNdamental Fitness is a series of yoga poses, strength training movements, and cardio exercises. It is a blending of styles that can challenge every body, every age, and every fitness level. It was created after years of studying functional fitness, yoga, Pilates, and cardio training...and personally experimenting and discovering what combinations made me, and my clients feel the best. In sharing these movements with my clients, I have watched them face fears, laugh at themselves, and grow to develop their own knowledge base of fitness for a lifelong plan of feeling good. I have also watched their bodies, their moods, and their energy change!

I searched for a model of fitness that represented the feeling I got when I did these exercises. Who effortlessly and exuberantly feels good? Who naturally performs physical movements with perfect form...no thinking? Who laughs while they work? Who keeps life simple and basic?

Well...athletes do some of this, but they are trained. Dancers look like they feel this way, but they are trained.

Who does it naturally, inherently?
CHILDREN DO.

As you read and open yourself up to the FUNdamentals in these pages, use the
pictures of the children as inspiration. Notice their form, their courage, their happiness.
When you combine these movements with the energy and desire of your youth,
allow it to trigger all areas of your wellbeing:

- Emotional…I am HAPPY.
- Spiritual…I am on my own path of wellness, and thankful for it.
- Nutritional…I am eating and supplementing my body to support my new actions and my new metabolism.
- Mental…I am thinking only thoughts that support me throughout this workout, and throughout my day.
- Physical…I am moving every day and using *FUNdamental Fitness* as a blueprint to challenge my body and make my workouts fun and kid-like.

And best of all…you are taking action. This alone triggers the body to respond.
It may just be the key to awaken others around you who need balancing…
welcome them! You are on a mission to feel good. And by feeling good,
you are inspiring others, perhaps even your own children now, to feel good.
Be brave, take action, spread the energy.

 Are you ready to be FUNdamentally FIT?

❀ ❀ ❀ ❀ ❀ ❀ ❀ ❀ ❀ ❀ ❀ ❀

PART TWO

BUILDING THE
FUNdamental FITNESS
WORKOUT

WHAT IS THE *FUNdamental Fitness* WORKOUT?

FUNdamental Fitness begins with a 5-minute WARMUP.
The muscles get loose and the mind gets ready!

Then we use YOGA to develop flexibility and fluidity. The YOGA allows us to quiet the mind, focus the breath, and bring our attention inward…where the power is! It is also a great benchmark for noticing improvement. Your comfort level in the poses, and the depth to which you can comfortably hold them can improve daily. YOGA is a great way to see how fast your body responds to this work.

FUNdamental Fitness then uses *functional fitness* and The Five Movement concept of strength training. Over the last few years, functional fitness has come alive. We now realize that training with machines only has proven to be ineffective, and not very fun! We used to think that in order to gain strength, we had to specialize, and target each muscle and fatigue it. We built strength, but only in the primary muscles. This helped our chest get strong, but it did not help us crawl on the floor with our children. Now we know that muscles work in groups, and that by training them in groups, we exercise the *firing patterns for moving functionally*. We are training firing patterns! How natural, how instinctual, how reminiscent! By training movements and firing patterns, instead of muscles, we begin to improve coordination, stability, AND strength! The machines were causing us to move like machines, not like athletes, and certainly not like children.

The Five Movements: SIT, PUSH, PULL, PRESS, and CURL, target each of the primary and secondary muscle groups. These basic movements of muscle groups are easily remembered and assimilated by the body. Who doesn't remember how to crawl, throw, jump, skip, or play tug-of-war? And by adding weights, repetitions, and joy, we can simulate a lot of what happened when we weren't thinking about it... when exercise was *play*!

SIT

PULL

For variety and challenge, *FUNdamental Fitness* then combines the Five Movements into TOTAL BODY MOVEMENTS or TBM. These movements work on balance, stability and coordination... oh, and a little cardio!

PUSH

CURL

And, for extra credit, we add a 2-minute cardio interval at the end. This is optional, but very fun, and very functional.

We do the YOGA poses again, for a cooldown. Here is where you notice any improvements in flexibility and range of motion.

PRESS

An EXERTION SCALE is included with this workout. It is purely a guide to relate the body to the workout. Practice getting in touch with how hard your body is working. Notice the difference between how hard you are trying, and how hard the muscles are actually working. This is a fine line, and becomes more obvious, the more in touch you become with your body. Trying is stress around the effort. It doesn't build muscle. Effort builds muscle. Find your unique scale and enjoy your workout accordingly!

Although no equipment is necessary, a Swiss Ball (see the box for appropriate size), a 4-6 lb. medicine ball, an exercise band with handles, and 3-10 lb. weights, can really open the door to tons of choices and challenges.

Let *FUNdamental Fitness* awaken you.
Bring back to life the way you instinctively move.
Release the child in you. Strengthen the grownup in you.

When did we stop feeling like kids?
When we stopped moving like them.
Enjoy these moves. Watch yourself while you do them, for symmetry, for a relaxed face…
Then close your eyes.
   Breathe.
    Get the view from the inside.

Building the *FUNdamental Fitness* Workout.

Here we go.
Anywhere.
A playground. Your backyard. Your living room. The gym.

FUNdamental Fitness is a go-anywhere, work-everything circuit:
a dancing WARMUP; grateful, stretching YOGA; 5 strength movements
(SIT, PUSH, PULL, PRESS, and CURL); Total Body Movements; and Cardio. It is simple.
The circuit takes about 15 minutes. Do it once, twice, or three times, every other day.

It is important to remember that all of these exercises work more than one muscle at a
time, and often more than one muscle *group* at a time! While learning these movements,
be patient with yourself. The plan is to eventually fatigue the PUSH muscles in the PUSH,
but in the early stages, your legs may get tired before your chest and arms do. In the SIT,
your core may fatigue faster than your legs or buns. This is perfectly fine. As grownups,
many of us have neglected doing some of these movements, and some muscles will
be new to this. Be aware of what gets tired first, and even make a note of it.
Then, in the next session, pay close attention to the *target* muscle groups, the muscles
you really want to work. Think of the abdominal muscles in the CURL. Send your
energy there. This focus can alleviate some of the imbalances, and often allow you
to relax the muscles that are trying too hard to help…(the neck or lower back muscles
in a CURL). But don't be disappointed if it takes a few sessions for some parts to catch up.
They will!

Repetition with great form is the key to getting results!

FUNdamental Fitness is a blueprint.
It is designed to give you basic movements with a ladder of increasing difficulty
and challenge. Once you have the *concept* of SIT, PUSH, PULL, PRESS, and CURL,
and feel comfortable that you are maintaining great form, you are free to expand
and invent your own exercises within these movements. The choices within this concept
are endless! As you get stronger, your choices get wider. But the basics are always
good to come back to and practice.

FUNdamental Fitness is designed to work the entire body, so doing this circuit *every other day* is ideal. The rest days can be used to cross-train with outdoor activities or rest!

Whether you do *FUNdamental Fitness* every other day or once a week, it is fun to start with your favorite exercises. In the workbook, circle your favorite PUSH, your favorite PULL, etc...and really get comfortable with the motions and muscles. After about three workouts, circle new exercises. Master those. After three more sessions, mix and match your first and second choices. This allows you to build your foundation of body and mind awareness about each movement. As your strength grows, so does your confidence and creativity.

It is important to get solid with each of the movements, so that you are working more than you are reading! Trust your instincts, use a mirror if possible...or ask a friend if your form looks like the descriptions in the book. And be honest with yourself. Know when you need to work a little harder, and truly know when to stop and rest.

FUNdamental Fitness *is designed to give you a total body training session in about 15 minutes. The first few times may take a little longer as you learn the movements and read the form tips, but soon you will be circling your choices and on your way in minutes!*

The *FUNdamental Fitness* Workout goes like this:

5 minute WARMUP...*anything goes...exertion level 1-5*

YOGA...*sun salute X 3...exertion level 3-4*

SIT...*8-15 reps...exertion level 5-6*
        Rest 30 seconds

PUSH...*8-15 reps...exertion level 5-6*
        Rest 30 seconds

PULL...*8-15 reps...exertion level 5-6*
        Rest 30 seconds

PRESS...*8-15 reps...exertion level 5-6*
        Rest 30 seconds

CURL...*8-15 reps...exertion level 5-6*
        Rest 30 seconds

TOTAL BODY MOVEMENT...*8-15 reps...exertion level 6-8*

CARDIO...*2 minutes...exertion level 6-10*

COOL DOWN, *add the YOGA again at the end. 3 breaths per pose!*

Here's what the *FUNdamental Fitness* Workout looks like in the Workbook.
Circle your choices, and fill in the blank (number of repetitions, weights, equipment).
The exercises are described in the FUNdamentals section, and page numbers are
next to the movements for easy reference.

FUNdamental Fitness takes approximately 15-20 minutes to complete, and the body
has been stretched and strengthened, *and* you have burned calories! By keeping
the exertion level between 6 and 7, the body stays in a target heart rate zone.
You are getting strength training and cardio training at the same time!

You may feel so wonderful after the first circuit, that you choose to do it again!
FUNdamental Fitness is a template that fits your energy level, and your time frame.
Do the circuit once, and see how you feel…if you feel energized…do it again! If you have
the time and the energy, do it one more time! Whether it is one, two, or three times
through the workout, you will train the entire body. The more you do it, the more calories
you burn, and the harder you strength train.

Take a deep breath and begin planning your *FUNdamental Fitness* Workout!

❀ ❀ ❀ ❀ ❀ ❀ ❀ ❀ ❀ ❀ ❀ ❀

FUNdamental Fitness WORKOUT

WARMUP

YOGA - 3x's PG. 25 - 29

_____ SIT

_____ PUSH

_____ PULL

_____ PRESS

_____ CURL

_____ TBM

_____ CARDIO

YOGA - 3x's PG. 25 - 29

TODAY IS _____

I DID THE CIRCUIT ___ TIMES

IT TOOK ME _____ MINUTES

I FEEL _____!

SIT
WALL SQUAT
MOVING SQUAT
SWISS BALL SQUAT
BACKWARD LUNGE
FORWARD LUNGE
BACK & FORWARD LUNGE
SIT AND LUNGE
SQUAT JUMP
ON YOUR MARK!
} PG. 35 - 47

PUSH
PUSH UP
PUSH UP W/POWER
PLANK
MOVING PLANK
SWISS BALL WALKOUTS
GI JOE (THE CRAWL)
MEDICINE BALL TOSS
YOGA PUSHUPS
} PG. 49 - 61

PULL
WATER SKIER
PIZZA PAN
CROSS COUNTRY SKIER
ONE ARM ROW
TWO ARM ROW
FLIES
SKI POLING
BAR SQUAT PULLUP
BAR ANGLE PULL
BAR JUMP PULLUP
} PG. 63 - 73

PRESS
MEDICINE BALL TOSS UP
MB SQUAT & TOSS UP
MOUNTAIN CLIMBER
FLOOR JACKS
SIDE TO SIDE PRESS
HANDSTAND
PALMS FACING PRESS
PALMS FACE OUT PRESS
PALMS IN PRESS
} PG. 75 - 85

CURL
123 CRUNCH
REVERSE CRUNCH
BACK EXTENSIONS
SEATED TWIST
SIDE CURLS
MEDICINE BALL LO TO HI
180° +
THE "X"
TICK-TOCK
SINGLE LEG STRETCH
SWIMMER
BICYCLE
BALLET EXTENSIONS
} PG. 87 - 103

TBM
MATRIX I, II, III
SQUAT PRESS
YOGA AIRPLANE
BURPEE!
BURPEE EXTRA!
} PG. 105 - 111

CARDIO
SKIP
JUMP ROPE
STEP UP/DOWN
WALK BRISKLY
JOG LIGHTLY
JUMPING JACKS
} PG. 112

PART THREE

THE
FUNdamentals

THE EXERTION SCALE

This number system is a way of measuring how hard you are working, and it gives you a guide to how hard you should be working. Everyone's 1-10 is unique, but the ratio of easy to hard is the same. You must work to your own level, but use this as a guide to keep you on track!

1
2
3 } Warmup/Cooldown Zone
4
5

TARGET TRAINING ZONE

The Five Movements and the Total Body Movements train at this level.

6 medium...heart rate begins to rise

7 medium hard...breathing increases...heart rate is strong

8 extra medium hard...breathing and heart rate are powerful

9 Hard! For advanced exercisers.

10 30-60 second maximum exertion

THE WARMUP

Warm muscles move easier, safer, and with more range-of-motion than cold muscles.
As grownups, it is important to send a signal to the cells, the muscles, the entire *body*,
to prepare for movement. Children, because of their natural anabolic (youthful) metabolism,
are always in *ready* mode, so they are pretty much warmed up all of the time.
Grownups need to reconnect with their muscles and joints, and prepare them for
some exertion. So…imagine yourself as 6 years old, put on some great music,
and tell the body that you are ready to begin!

Pick two favorite songs that make you feel alive…
                    and dance!
Start with small movements, gradually widening them.

Do a body check…
            Have I moved my toes? My ankles? Bent my knees?
            Have I kicked forward? Bent forward? Looked up?
            Reached up? If you really remembered being 6 years old,
            then everything moved at least a little!

Another way to warm up the body is to use the Exertion Scale. Imagine increasing your
efforts by one level, every minute. Take your body from exertion level 1 (watching TV)…
to level 5 (walking briskly around the block).

In the warmup, you will use levels 1- 5.
            1st minute…walk in place using big arms
            2nd minute…walk around house or yard
            3rd minute…lift knees in place
            4th minute…walk pressing arms overhead
            5th minute…walk up stairs 2-3 times

Do you feel that there is more oxygen in the brain and muscles now?
There is. Now it is time to lengthen and train the muscles for flexibility and
range-of-motion.

Be creative.
Be good to yourself.

YOGA

Practice these poses with a gentle mind.
The stretching is perfect...animals (and children)
do it so naturally!

YOGA

The body is warm.
Be grateful for its ability to move in all directions, easily and happily.
These yoga poses open energy pathways in the body, allowing receptivity and an openness to new strength and new ideas.

Yoga is also a great marker for flexibility and range-of-motion.
Every time you do the poses (in the warmup and cool down), notice your comfort level, your strength, and your ease with the motion. The more you do these poses, the more beautiful and joyous you become.

Once you feel confident about the yoga poses, and can string them together from memory, add conscious breathing to the work. Breathe through your nose, if you can, and be aware of exhaling on the hardest part of the motion. Hold the poses for 3 full breaths, and transition on the exhale. You'll get the hang of it after you do it a few times. Get the poses first, then synchronize your breathing.

This combination of poses is a modified Sun Salutation. It is a greeting to above, below, side-to-side, forward, and back. So, pretend you are 5 years old, joyous and thankful to be here...and stretch!

THE SUN SALUTATION

Body tall…feet, knees, and buns firm and strong.
Look to the sky, hands up and together. Be as tall as you can.
Inhale…as you exhale, gently "tick tock" your body from side to side, 2-3 times.
On the third time hold it right for 3 breaths, then left. On an exhale, return to center.
Feel your waist up through your fingertips awaken.

Tick Tock

At the center, look up and then trace your eyes and your fingers behind you, bending from the waist, up and over the ribcage. Allow your front to lengthen, and your back to slightly bend. Breathe 2-3 times, exhale and stand.

Backward Bend

Keeping your head between your arms, round your body down, folding into your legs. Feel the back of your legs lengthen, and your spine stretch. Don't lock your knees!

Forward Bend

Bend the knees, and with your hands, walk or crawl yourself out to a pushup (plank) position. Breathe 2-3 times.

As slow as you can, lower yourself until you are flat on the ground.
It is okay to lower your knees first, and then the rest of your body, but try not to bend from your knees to the top of your head! Feel the strength in your chest and arms as practice lowering slower and slower. (Exhale as you lower).

Plank

Point your toes away from you, and squeezing your buns, gently raise your chest off the floor, looking up to the sky. Use your elbows or hands to extend the stretch. Breathe 3 times.

Cobra

Lower your chest to the ground, flex the balls of your feet into the ground, and (on an exhale), push your tailbone into the air, walking the hands back a little. Push your heels toward the floor and your push your head between your arms. Feel your shoulders and hamstrings lengthen.

Down Dog

Bend the knees and walk the hands toward the feet. Keep your head down and roll the body to standing...beautiful!

Try the sun salutation again...in a flow.
Think tall, and long.
Feel strong and relaxed.
Exhale on the pose changes, and breathe in and out three times per pose.

STAND TALL, TICK TOCK, BACKWARD BEND, FORWARD BEND.
CRAWL TO PLANK, LOWER DOWN, ARCH UP INTO COBRA.
LOWER DOWN, TAILBONE UP, INTO DOWN DOG.
BEND THE KNEES, WALK BACK TO FORWARD BEND,
ROLL UP. SMILE.

Now...do the sun salutation once more...try closing your eyes.

❄ ❄ ❄ ❄ ❄ ❄ ❄ ❄ ❄ ❄ ❄ ❄

*Imagine yourself
healthy and strong.*

THE FIVE MOVEMENTS

THE FIVE MOVEMENTS

Here's where you build strength.

SIT, PUSH, PULL PRESS, CURL, are Five Movements that target all of the main muscle groups. Groups means the major muscle plus the surrounding muscles, *plus* any additional muscles in the "firing pattern" that are needed for stability and support. Whew!

> For example... at the gym, the chest press machine uses chest muscles and some arm and shoulder muscles.
>
> In a PUSH movement (let's use the pushup), a similar action occurs with the upper body, *but now the lower body and the core are working and strengthening too.*

By using mostly your own body weight, adding unstable surfaces, small weights, and power (acceleration), the body is strengthened and challenged, the way it is in normal, everyday life. Kids train their bodies with naturally perfect form, instinctively...as they *play*... Grownups need a few tips and reminders on how the body is supposed to work.

It is vital to train motions that we use in normal life. Kids are training functionally all day long, with ease. For grownups, bench pressing 200 pounds is strong...but not being able to crawl across the floor with your children is not strong. If we train our bodies to move functionally, and watch the children for inspiration and perfect form, we will be well on our way to a safe, **FUN,** and successful fitness program!

This chapter will go through each of the Five Movements to find your starting point, your challenging point, and your endurance factor. It is important to start easy, find which version of the exercise will allow you to maintain great form, and be able to do 8-15 repetitions. If you can do more than 15 repetitions, make it tougher.

> *If you can do 8-12 repetitions while maintaining great form...fantastic.*
> *If you can't, go back and make the movement a little easier. Great form is crucial in order to train the correct firing patterns of the muscle groups...the instinctive actions that keep us strong and safe.*

Study the various exercises for each movement, and feel which ones are perfectly challenging for you. Then circle those movements in the workbook, and as you go through each movement, you will have a tailor-made program of functional strength training!

These movements are designed to be practiced anywhere. Make your living room a gym, or make the gym a playground, or go outside and surround yourself with the experts. Remember that we are retraining the firing patterns with the Five Movements... allowing the body to react and train instinctively and youthfully! Feel the **FUN!**

SIT

PULL

PRESS

PUSH

CURL

This is fun!

THE SIT

Whenever you sit down and stand up,
you are performing this movement.
It targets the entire lower body, including the lower back!

THE SIT

The SIT is a natural movement that happens every time we sit down or stand up, step up or down, jump, or squat. This action targets the entire lower body: the quadriceps, hamstrings, upper thighs, calves, and buns. The core also plays a crucial role in this movement.

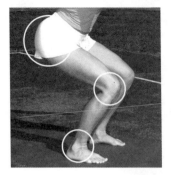

Every time we SIT, whether the motion occurs with one leg or two legs, we are technically increasing or decreasing the angles of the hip joints, the knees and the ankles.
In every SIT, it is important to pay close attention to the alignment of these three spots.

We SIT hundreds of times every day, so to strengthen these muscles, we will use these positions:

SQUAT…
2 LEGS

LUNGE…
1 LEG

COMBO
& POWER!

AT THE GYM…

THE SQUAT
LEG PRESS
DEADLIFT

Let's establish great SIT form!

Keep in mind that we were fantastic at the SIT as children, and we do it all day long now.
Let's make sure we are doing it in the strongest, safest way!

- Whether on one leg or two, the feet, ankles, knees, and hips are all in line.
The shoulders line up over the ankles.
This provides a stable foundation for the SIT muscles to work.

- Body weight is grounded in mostly the *heels* of the feet.
The toes are spread, the feet are relaxed.

- The spine is neutral/natural, or slightly arched. NOT ROUNDED!

- The core is strong and supportive. Exhale on the hardest part of the exercise—
pulling back up to standing.

In the SIT movement, the goal is to keep great form in order to strengthen the
lower body. Because we are using the biggest muscle groups in the body, it takes
more effort. Don't be surprised if your heart rate gets up on these exercises...
you are burning extra calories *and* increasing strength!

The SIT works best by following this progression:
Establish great form with the SQUAT. Start without weights, and as your strength and
stability increase, *and great form is maintained,* increase your repetitions from 8-15.
If this is comfortable and stable, you can learn the LUNGE choices. Once again, start
without weights, and as you perfect your form and stability, add weight and repetitions.
Start with 5 per leg and work up to 15 per leg!
Then you can learn the COMBO/POWER movements.

The SIT foundation, when learned with two legs first, then one leg, then power,
will bring you the greatest results.

The muscles that enable you to jump, sprint, and leap
are known as the POWER SOURCE, of the body.
Kids and kangaroos are famous for this!

✲ ✲ ✲ ✲ ✲ ✲ ✲ ✲ ✲ ✲ ✲

Let's work the SIT…
        The SQUAT…2 LEGS
                The LUNGE…1 LEG
                        And the COMBO/POWER

THE SQUAT...2 LEGS!

THE WALL SQUAT

The WALL SQUAT is a static version of the perfect squat form.
Once we establish great form, we can use the wall to deepen the SIT, and perfect
the form. The wall can help take some of the effort away from the lower back,
allowing you to work a little deeper and a little longer.
Keeping your weight on your heels, lean slightly forward from the hips, and press
your sitbones against the wall. Your arms can be extended, or next to the body.
Slowly work your way down to a 90° angle at the knee joint, always keeping
a slight arch in the lower back.
Time yourself. Work up to one minute!

THE MOVING SQUAT...

Using great SIT form, and now *no* wall, start with the feet shoulder-width apart, knees over the feet, and hips over the knees. SIT the buns back, shifting your weight to the heels, and creating a slight arch in the spine. Tighten your stomach muscles to support the spine. Then SIT! Count 1-2-3, then stand on 4. Breathe in on the 1-2-3, breathe out on the 4. Start with 5-8 of these. Add 3-8lb weights or a medicine ball as you get stronger, if your form can stay stable (usually that means when you can keep that slight arch in the spine throughout the movement).

Squat 1, 2, 3...

Stand 4...
don't lock the knees!

With Medicine Ball

Be thankful for your body.
Enjoy it. Love it

THE SWISS BALL SQUAT...

The SWISS BALL SQUAT combines the WALL SQUAT and the MOVING SQUAT. Place an appropriately sized swiss ball (the recommendations are usually on the box) against a solid wall.
Place your lower back against the ball. Practice the squat as you check your toe/knee/hip alignment, and slight arch in the spine. Feel yourself supported throughout the moving squat.
Start with 5 reps, and increase to 15.

*Notice how often the SIT happens naturally throughout the day.
Remind yourself of great SIT form, and you will be exercising all day long...imagine!*

✵ ✵ ✵ ✵ ✵ ✵ ✵ ✵ ✵ ✵ ✵ ✵

TIPS!

• *Squeeze your buns to stand.*
• *Exhale on the hard part.*
• *Can you tap your toes throughout the movement?*
• *Is your lower back slightly arched at the bottom of the SIT?*

✵ ✵ ✵ ✵ ✵ ✵ ✵ ✵ ✵ ✵ ✵ ✵

Once you are comfortable with the SQUATS,
challenge yourself with the LUNGE, or the ONE-LEG SQUAT.
The same form principles for the 2 LEG SQUAT apply here.
It helps to start in the SQUAT position and LUNGE from there.
Try these:

BACKWARD LUNGE

From standing, move one leg back, keeping the weight over the stationary leg.
SIT using mostly the front leg, making sure that the front shinbone stays perpendicular
to the floor. Stand, using mostly the front leg again. Stick your buns out.
Repeat the LUNGE on one side 8-15 times. Then LUNGE backward on the other side,
the same number of times.

If balance is a challenge, try gently holding
on to the back of a chair. Practice using whole
hand, then 4 fingers, then 3, 2, then 1!
Often, 1 finger is just enough support to
stabilize the LUNGE!

THE FORWARD LUNGE!

Start with the feet, knees and hips in line. Pretend you are wearing
skis…this will keep you lined up throughout the movement.
Step forward with the right leg, stopping the forward motion
when the shin becomes perpendicular to the floor.
Keeping the upper body tilted forward, lower yourself with
the buns of the forward leg. The weight is mostly in the heel
of the front foot. Push back to starting position.
Do 8-15 times on each side.

THE BACK AND FORWARD LUNGE!

Combine the above 2 lunges, and you get an exercise that challenges the buns, quads, hamstrings, calves, lower back, AND balance!
Start with the BACKWARD LUNGE, and return to a stand. Then FORWARD LUNGE with the same leg. That is one repetition. Start with 5 reps on each side. You can lightly hold on to the back of a chair until you are comfortable. As you get stronger, try not touching the foot down in between LUNGES! Switch legs.

Wear bright colors.
Don't care what others think...kids don't!
Ask your inner 8-year old what (s)he wants to do today. Do it.

When you feel stable on the SQUATS and LUNGES,
and your form is great throughout the movement, you are ready for:

COMBO/POWER LUNGES

THE SIT AND LUNGE!

Start in a SQUAT. Stand. Do a FORWARD LUNGE with the right leg.
Push back to standing. SQUAT. Stand. LUNGE forward with the left leg.
Push back to standing. SQUAT. That is one repetition. Start with 5 reps, and work up to 10.
Keep the form perfect as you add speed or light weights.

*TIP! You can place
your hands on the
knee of the forward
moving leg for balance
and concentration.
Use a wall to SQUAT
against, if you feel
it helps the stability.*

THE SQUAT JUMP!

This movement is all about the power source! This will raise that heart rate, so try 5, rest,
and try 5 more. Work your way up to 10, then 15.

SQUAT…   Jump…   Land in a SQUAT.

When doing power moves, we are essentially jumping. Keep in mind great sit form throughout the jump…push off heel to toe…land toe to heel, as gently as you can. Remember…this is fun!

ON YOUR MARK!

This movement is a stationary LUNGE with power.
Start with a FORWARD LUNGE. Bending over from the hips, touch the ground, like the start of a race, back is flat. Keeping the weight on the forward leg, stand. Bend mostly at the knee, not at the waist. Do 8-10 on each leg. If you feel strong, add power, but be sure to land gently, toe to heel.
Start with 5 on each leg. Work up to 10!

On your mark! Press to standing. Add power!

❄ ❄ ❄ ❄ ❄ ❄ ❄ ❄ ❄ ❄ ❄ ❄

TIPS!

• *Jump higher as you get stronger.*
• *Keep your eyes straight ahead for the best alignment.*

❄ ❄ ❄ ❄ ❄ ❄ ❄ ❄ ❄ ❄ ❄ ❄

Let the kid in you shine!

Practice these movements with and without weights.
Close your eyes when you are comfortable.
Try them on a trampoline for extra, extra credit!
Have fun!

❋ ❋ ❋ ❋ ❋ ❋ ❋ ❋ ❋ ❋ ❋ ❋

Choose one SIT and circle it in the FUNdamental WORKBOOK
You have begun to chart your personal program of *FUNdamental Fitness.*

5 minutes of WARMUP

YOGA...SUN SALUTATION...3 x's

SIT
Your choices are:

SQUAT	WALL SQUAT
	MOVING SQUAT
	SWISS BALL SQUAT
LUNGE	BACK LUNGE
	FORWARD LUNGE
	BACK AND FORWARD LUNGE
COMBO/ POWER	SIT AND LUNGE
	SQUAT JUMP
	ON YOUR MARK!

> *Learn the SQUAT first,*
> *Then the LUNGE,*
> *Then COMBO/POWER!*
> *When you have*
> *learned them all,*
> *mix and match,*
> *increase the reps,*
> *or add weight!*

Eat when you are hungry,
stop eating when you
are no longer hungry.
Fall in love with water
and drink tons of it!
Move every day.

THE PUSH

This movement focuses on the chest muscles,
while engaging the shoulder girdle, the core, and the triceps.

THE PUSH

In the PUSH, the elbows begin out and away from the body, then move toward the center front of the body. Kids would never describe a push like that, so let's just practice the concept of this:

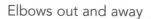

Elbows out and away

Elbows in front and center…

Every time we push something away:

THE WALL...

THE FLOOR...

A BALL...

AT THE GYM...

BENCH PRESS

BENCH FLIES

INCLINE BENCH PRESS

DECLINE BENCH PRESS

...we are technically moving the elbow joints from out and away from the body...
into the center of the body. The PUSH uses chest muscles, shoulder muscles, triceps,
and sometimes the real center of the body...the core!

Let's establish great PUSH form:

• The feet (toes) are in line with the knees, knees in line with hips.
Knees are soft (not locked, and not bent).

• The spine is natural/neutral...that means not rounded,
and not too arched.

• Shoulders are strong, and pressed towards the waist.
Shrug your shoulders up, then relax them down...keep that strong.
That is a good shoulder girdle stance.

• Elbows are allowed to be anywhere from right next to the body,
to just below shoulder level.

Changing the elbow/arm position from next to the body, to just below shoulder level,
allows more angles and choices to challenge and strengthen the muscles.

Are you ready to find your PUSH starting exercises?

In these three main exercises, the goal is to keep great form, and challenge yourself
enough to increase strength.

Let's work the PUSHUP...
            THE PLANK...
                    And THE MEDICINE BALL TOSS!

❊ ❊ ❊ ❊ ❊ ❊ ❊ ❊ ❊ ❊ ❊

THE PUSHUP

Determine your PUSHUP strength.

Start with the WALL PUSHUP...

Stand upright, an arm's length away from a wall or pole. With great PUSH form, not bending anything from your toes to your head, move the elbows away from the centerline of the body, lowering the body to the wall. Then, like a 5-year-old, PUSH away from the wall. Do this 8-15 times. Exertion level is 5. If this is easy, add power...

Push

away

with power!

As the WALL PUSHUP becomes easy, lower the wall…then add power!

The couch PUSHUP…

OR

The chair PUSHUP, on the knees.

Remember! If you can do 15 pushups, it is time to increase the difficulty!
The last few reps in the set should be tough!

THE PLANK

The PLANK is a major PUSH exercise that engages the chest, shoulder girdle, arms, core, and legs. A quick review of proper PUSH form, reminds us that

- Feet, knees and hips are in line and not locked.
- The spine is neutral…no flexing or rounding.
- Shoulders are strong and pressed toward the waist.
- Elbows/hands are directly under the shoulders.
- The pelvis is slightly tucked under, crunching the core for support.

Hold this position for 10, 20, 30 seconds. Rest for 30 seconds. Repeat. This static movement solidifies the shoulder girdle and arms, and strengthens the abdominals and lower back. Exertion level 6.

Once you can hold this plank for 30 seconds, you are ready to increase the difficulty! Keeping the hips and shoulders in place, lift your right hand a few inches… hold for 4 seconds. Switch hands. Then try lifting one foot at a time. Maintaining a strong PLANK position, and keeping the hips and shoulders in perfect PLANK form, are the real challenges.

Alternate R & L arms 8 x's, then R & L legs 8 x's. REST 30 sec.
Repeat. Exertion level 7.

THE MOVING PLANK

Here's where you really start to feel like a kid.
From a perfect plank position, bend the knees slightly and walk your hands to your feet, keeping the tailbone down. Then walk your hands right back out, to a plank!
You are doing half of a crawl!

Do 5-12 of these, depending on your fitness level.
Do them in slow motion for added strength training. (Exertion level 7)
Do them fast for more cardio! (Exertion level 8)

THE SWISS BALL WALKOUT

If the PLANK feels good, and the MOVING PLANK feels good, adding an unstable surface takes everything up a notch!

Keeping great PLANK form, crouch in front of an exercise ball appropriate for your height (check the box), and round over it, placing the hands on the opposite side.
Keeping the shoulders strong and shrugged toward the waist, the core solid,
and the pelvis slightly tucked under…walk your body away from the ball!
If your middle is sagging, or your shoulders are rounding you've gone too far out!
Walk the hands back in.

> *It is easier to stabilize on the ball if the legs are slightly apart.*
> *Also: Scan your exercise area for objects that you don't want to fall into or on…*
> *this is an easy one to bounce around with.*

Walkout 5-12 times, keeping great form. Exertion level 6.
The farther out you walk, the more challenging it is!

THE GI JOE... (THE CRAWL)

You are now officially 6 years old.

In a great moving plank position, keeping knees and elbows slightly bent, CRAWL forward 10 steps, then backward 10 steps.

Rest 30 seconds.

Repeat 2 more times. Watch the experts for tips on form and speed...

Exertion level 7-8.

Practice the energy of a child.
Crawl with them, jump with them, swing with them.
Exercise with children...they LOVE it!

THE MEDICINE BALL TOSS

This is where the kid in you comes alive!

With a 4-6 pound medicine ball, and keeping great PUSH form, stand a couple of feet from a solid brick wall and toss the ball against it.

You are playing catch with yourself!

This PUSH challenges the entire body, plus hand-eye coordination.

Throw for 1 minute, (30 throws).
Rest 30 seconds. Repeat.
Exertion level 6.

For extra challenge, throw with a friend.
Throw it high, or wide, or on one leg,
for more work, and more fun!
Throw 30, rest 30 sec., repeat.

❋ ❋ ❋ ❋ ❋ ❋ ❋ ❋ ❋ ❋ ❋ ❋

TIP!

Pay attention to right and left hands PUSHing evenly.
The dominant hand tends to dominate!

❋ ❋ ❋ ❋ ❋ ❋ ❋ ❋ ❋ ❋ ❋ ❋

The last PUSH exercise is my favorite...
THE YOGA PUSHUP

This exercise combines the plank with the knee pushup.
Essentially, this trains half of a genuine PUSHup!

Do 5-12 of these. As you get stronger, use less and less knees.

❋ ❋ ❋ ❋ ❋ ❋ ❋ ❋ ❋ ❋ ❋
TIPS!

*Increase the difficulty by using the knees less and less,
eventually doing a full pushup.
Vary your elbow position from just below the shoulder, to next to the body.*

❋ ❋ ❋ ❋ ❋ ❋ ❋ ❋ ❋ ❋ ❋

Now that you have determined your strength level on the different PUSH exercises, pick your favorite and circle it in the FUNdamental WORKBOOK section in the back.

5 minutes of WARMUP...*dancing, walking, reaching/bending*

YOGA...SUN SALUTATION...3x's

SIT

PUSH
Your choices are:

PUSH UP (wall, couch, chair on knees)

PUSH UP WITH POWER (wall, couch, chair)

PLANK (hold for 10, 20, 30...pick up arm, leg)

MOVING PLANK (on floor)

SWISS BALL WALKOUTS

GI JOE (THE CRAWL)

MEDICINE BALL TOSS (wall, or with partner)

YOGA PUSHUP

Soreness is good.
Pain is not.

THE PULL

This movement focuses on all of the muscles in the back,
while working the shoulders and biceps too.

THE PULL

The PULL movement is the opposite of the PUSH. The PULL moves the elbows from "out and away from" the body, toward the center "back" of the body. The main purpose of the PULL is to squeeze the shoulder blades together. This squeeze engages the muscles of the back, shoulders and arms.

Elbows out and away

Elbows and shoulders squeezing back

When we PULL, we can use resistance to challenge the muscles. Here are the tools:

A BAND

A BAR

LIGHT
WEIGHTS

AT THE GYM...
LAT PULLDOWN
2 ARM SEATED ROW
1 ARM ROW
PULLBACKS
REAR DELT FLIES
ETC...

Now let's establish great PULL form!

• Stand up, relaxed, arms by your sides. Shrug your shoulders up as if saying "I don't know". Then shrug them down and back, solidly. This shrug establishes a firm "shoulder girdle", protecting the more delicate muscles inside the shoulder joint.

• Keeping the shoulder girdle solid, extend your arms out in front of you. Imagine there is a large walnut between your shoulder blades, and using only your shoulders, crack the walnut! (arms stay straight for now).

• Once you feel your shoulders moving independently of your arms, add the elbows moving back to increase the crunch.

• The motion of the scapula (shoulder blades) is the first step in creating a perfect PULL…the elbows increase the squeeze.

Arms extended   Shoulders squeeze back   Elbows finish the squeeze

The following exercises are shown with an overhand grip.
To intensify the exercise and challenge the body, try an underhand grip too!

In these three main PULL exercises, the goal is to keep great form, and to challenge yourself enough to increase strength. One set of 8-15 reps is perfect. Exertion level 6-7.

Let's PULL using The BAND...
LIGHT WEIGHTS...
And the BAR...

❋ ❋ ❋ ❋ ❋ ❋ ❋ ❋ ❋ ❋ ❋

THE BAND

The use of an elastic band, preferably one with handles, adds great resistance for the PULL! Find a pole, a tree, or a friend to act as a ground. Wrap the band around, and step back far enough to stretch your shoulder blades apart. Assume great PULL stance with feet shoulder width apart, knees bent and in line with the hips, and back flat or slightly arched. (if you have ever water skied, this is the stance!) Feel yourself standing straighter and prouder as you feel your back, shoulders, and arms muscles strengthen!

WATER SKIER

Palms face
each other,
shoulders
are down.

Squeeze
shoulder blades
together. Hold.
Release slowly.

PIZZA PAN

Palms face down. Hands, elbows, shoulders so flat that you could carry a pizza on them, and not spill!

Squeeze shoulder blades together. Hold. Release slowly.

CROSS COUNTRY SKIER

Arms straight, palms face down. Bend slightly forward from the hips. PULL with your back muscles, extending the arms behind you.

Hold. Release slowly. Repeat 8-15 x's.

Remember, the main purpose of the PULL is to squeeze your shoulder blades together. Allow your back to arch, and your chest to come forward. Increase the difficulty by stepping back and increasing the resistance.

❋ ❋ ❋ ❋ ❋ ❋ ❋ ❋ ❋ ❋ ❋ ❋

TIPS!

• Remember to start the movement with the shoulders, and then finish the squeeze by moving the elbows.

• PULL with an exhale. Return slowly with an inhale.

• Keep the hands relaxed, so the energy stays in the PULL muscles.

For variety, try PULLing one arm at a time...or stand on one leg... you start really challenging your core and stabilizer muscles!

❋ ❋ ❋ ❋ ❋ ❋ ❋ ❋ ❋ ❋ ❋ ❋

LIGHT WEIGHTS:
ROWS, FLIES, and SKI POLING

These exercises are perfect with weights and without weights.
Use a mirror to perfect your form, and then close your eyes and feel the shoulder blades squeezing together. Don't add so much weight that you can't get the full range of motion. Start with 3-5lbs. in each hand. When you can do 12-15 repetitions without losing your form, go to 5-8lbs. Please remember to keep your knees bent and your chest slightly lifted in all of these exercises!

Bent over one arm rows

Bent over two arm rows.

Flies…

Shoulders stay
firm and steady.
Core stays strong
and supporting.

PULL arms forward
and backward
with purpose.
Try for great
range of motion.
Go slow, and
don't swing!

Ski poling

✽ ✽ ✽ ✽ ✽ ✽ ✽ ✽ ✽ ✽ ✽ ✽

TIPS!

• *Keep the great PULL form while in the bent stance.*
  Core stays strong, back stays slightly arched.

• *Exhale on the PULL, inhale on the release.*

• *If the lower back gets tired first, keep working without weights.*
  Add weight and repetitions as you get stronger!

• *Try these on one leg! Keep the hips in line, and back arched!*
  Go for it!

✽ ✽ ✽ ✽ ✽ ✽ ✽ ✽ ✽ ✽ ✽ ✽

THE BAR
THE BAR SQUAT PULLUP

PULL from a squat...

To a bar hang!

Any playground will have many sized bars to experiment with, or you can invent your own at home! Start with a bar about chest high. With an overhand grip, hang from the bar, allowing your legs to squat below you. Using great PULL form, shrug your shoulders down. Then use your back muscles and *only as much lower body muscles as you need,* PULL your chest toward the bar. Hold yourself up there for one breath. On an exhale, lower yourself down slowly. Repeat 8-15 times.

Keep in mind as you work toward a full PULLUP, your legs and butt will be getting a workout too! The stronger you become at this PULL, the less you will use your lower body. Be honest with yourself!

TIP!

Remember the physical fitness tests in gym class...the bar hang for girls, and the pullups for boys? Keeping the strength in the back and shoulder girdle, rather than the arms, allows you to last a lot longer!

THE BAR ANGLE PULL

For an extra challenge, find a bar waist high. Establish great PULL form with your body at an angle. Keep your body stiff, and PULL your chest toward the bar. Lower slowly. (The legs can't help you much here!)

Hang...squeeze shoulder blades

PULL chest toward bar.

The PULL's ultimate exercise is the PULLUP.
All of the previous exercises are strengthening the PULLUP muscles.
If the kid in you is ready, try this!

THE BAR JUMP PULLUP

Find a bar that is as high as your forehead.
Using overhand, or underhand grip,
jump up to a bar hang.
Squeezing the shoulder girdle, lower yourself to
a fully extended position, bending the knees
so you can lengthen yourself. This is fun!

Count out loud through the workout.
This allows the exhale to easily happen at the
right time & keeps you breathing!

❋ ❋ ❋ ❋ ❋ ❋ ❋ ❋ ❋ ❋ ❋

Now that you have determined your strength level
on the different PULL exercises,
circle one in the FUNdamental WORKBOOK!

5 minutes of WARMUP

YOGA...SUN SALUTATION...3 x's

SIT

PUSH

PULL
Your choices are:

THE WATER SKIER
THE PIZZA PAN
THE CROSS COUNTRY SKIER
BENT OVER ONE ARM ROWS
BENT OVER TWO ARM ROWS
FLIES
SKI POLING
THE BAR SQUAT PULLUP
THE BAR ANGLE PULL
THE BAR JUMP PULLUP

*Make up songs
while you move…
exercise your
brain too!*

THE PRESS

The shoulder girdle is the main ingredient in this
overhead movement. Often the entire body (including the core)
is challenged by the press.

THE PRESS

The PRESS is a PUSH overhead. A PRESS moves the elbows from next to the body, to out and away, and above the body.

Elbows out, away   and above!

Every time we PRESS something away:

A BALL

THE FLOOR

LIGHT WEIGHTS

AT THE GYM...
OVERHEAD PRESS MACHINE
PRESS WITH FREE WEIGHTS

...we are technically moving the elbows out, away, and above the body.
The PRESS uses mostly the shoulder muscles, but the arms, back, chest, legs, and core can be challenged with this movement!

Let's establish great PRESS form:

• The feet (toes) are in line with the knees which are in line with the hips.

• The spine is natural/neutral, not rounded, and perhaps slightly arched.

• Shoulders are strong and PRESSed toward the waist.
So shrug your shoulders up, and then relax them down.
Keep that strong and stable throughout these exercises.

• The elbows can be anywhere from beside the body
to in front of the body, at the start of the exercises.
Be sure the forearm stays parallel to the body.

Beside   Slightly in front   In front

Changing this arm/elbow position gives the PRESS more angles and choices
to challenge and strengthen the muscles.

❃ ❃ ❃ ❃ ❃ ❃ ❃ ❃ ❃ ❃ ❃ ❃

Don't lock out the elbows at the end of the PRESS.
This can lead to overstretching of the tendons and ligaments, and plus…
it is resting!! Try to keep the movement active!

❃ ❃ ❃ ❃ ❃ ❃ ❃ ❃ ❃ ❃ ❃ ❃

Are you ready to start PRESSing?

In these three main exercises, the goal is to keep great form, and challenge yourself enough to increase your strength.

Let's work THE BALL...
THE FLOOR...
and LIGHT WEIGHTS!

❋ ❋ ❋ ❋ ❋ ❋ ❋ ❋ ❋ ❋ ❋

THE BALL

THE MEDICINE BALL TOSS UP

The safest way to start this exercise is to practice it without the ball.
Start with your feet hip-distance apart, and hips, knees, and feet all in line.
Bend the knees slightly and keeping the shoulders shrugged down, straighten the knees (not locking them), and toss the imaginary ball into the air. Start with a small toss (about a foot), increase the height as you feel confident. Always watch the ball.
Catch it just above the head and let your knees slightly bend to the starting position.
The lower body essentially acts as a shock absorber! Now add a 2-4 lb ball.
Start with 8-15 repetitions. Increase the weight of the ball as you get stronger.
Do a maximum of 25 repetitions per set. Exertion level is 6.

The medicine ball will hurt if it hits you! Watch closely and have fun!

THE MEDICINE BALL SQUAT AND TOSS UP!

This exercise is exactly the same as the TOSS UP, but beginning and ending the exercise in a squat position. So the MB starts at knee level, the back is flat (or slightly arched, your buns stick out, so that you can always see your feet. PUSH with the heels to a standing position, while PUSHing/tossing the ball overhead. Catch and return to the squat position. Exertion level is 7.

Keep the PRESS, toss, catch, and squat, all one continuous motion. Find a rhythm and try not to stop between tosses.

✳ ✳ ✳ ✳ ✳ ✳ ✳ ✳ ✳ ✳ ✳ ✳

TIPS!

• *Keep your stance relaxed and in line.*
• *Maintain a continuous rhythm while tossing and catching.*
• *Can you toss it higher?*
• *Exhale on the PRESS, inhale on the catch.*
• *Pretend you are 6 years old!*

✳ ✳ ✳ ✳ ✳ ✳ ✳ ✳ ✳ ✳ ✳ ✳

THE FLOOR

The floor exercises really bring out the kid in you!

They are a cross between the "DOWN DOG" in yoga and "THE PLANK", in the PUSH section...only they *move!* The arms are overhead PRESSing against the floor, while the lower body jumps around, adding a bouncy kind of resistance. The heart rate can get going in these, so pace yourself and stop when you need to. Exertion level is 7.

> *Count to 16...that means that each leg moves 8 times, alternating.*
> *Rest for an equal 16 counts, then repeat! As you get stronger,*
> *increase the count to 20, then all the way to 30!*
> *Do you remember being 6 years old yet?*

✻ ✻ ✻ ✻ ✻ ✻ ✻ ✻ ✻ ✻

THE MOUNTAIN CLIMBER

With your palms on the floor and your fingers spread wide, use your strong shoulder girdle and core to put your tailbone in the air. Keeping the knees slightly bent, alternate the legs forward and back, allowing your feet to come off the floor about 2 inches. Keep the weight in your shoulders and hands. No locking elbows or locking knees. Breathe! Relax the neck. This is fun.

FLOOR JACKS

Keep the same position as the
MOUNTAIN CLIMBER, but jump
legs in and out. Remember to
Keep the knees and elbows soft.
Use 8 counts moving, 8 counts
Rest. Repeat.

SIDE TO SIDE PRESS

Keeping the same position as the above exercises, put your feet and knees together,
and jump them from SIDE TO SIDE. This exercise adds extra challenge to the core.
Start with 16 counts (alternating sides), and work your way up to 30 counts.

Play your favorite music.
Do it with a friend.
Do it outside as much as possible!

THE HANDSTAND!

This exercise is all about being a kid. You may not have been upside down in a while, so take it easy. You may want to have someone spot you. Don't skip this one... the sensation is wonderful, as is the challenge for your shoulder girdle and spirit!

Touch a solid wall with your tailbone. Bend over and place your hands on the ground, shoulder girdle shrugged down tight. Keeping the fingers spread wide, and the weight in your shoulders, carefully straighten one leg up the wall. Add the other leg, if you feel comfortable. Relax the neck and breathe 3 full breaths. Bend one leg to the floor, then the other to get down. Increase your time in the HANDSTAND as you improve. 3 breaths, 5 breaths, 10 breaths? Exertion level is 7.

❈ ❈ ❈ ❈ ❈ ❈ ❈ ❈ ❈ ❈ ❈

TIPS!

• *Are your fingers spread, sharing the energy?*
• *Is your shoulder girdle solid and shrugged down?*
• *Is the work happening mainly in your shoulders and arms?*
• *Is your core strong, supporting your lower back?*

❈ ❈ ❈ ❈ ❈ ❈ ❈ ❈ ❈ ❈ ❈

LIGHT WEIGHTS

THE OVERHEAD PRESS

These exercises are perfect for strengthening the shoulders, the back, and the arms. They are powerful because you can start with very little weight and can quickly notice the increase in strength. Start with 3 lb. weights. If you can do 15 reps, move up to 5's. If you can do 15 reps, move up to 8's, etc. All three exercises have the same lower body stance, so by varying the elbow position, you can challenge yourself in three totally different ways! Exertion level is 6.

Remember the PRESS form?
Feet are shoulder width apart...knees and hips are all in line.
Keep knees soft, and your spine neutral. Shoulders are shrugged down towards the body, and the wrists are straight (not flexed).
Forearms should always stay parallel to the body.
PRESS ON!

* * * * * * * * * * * * *

I. PALMS FACING PRESS

Using light weights, and NOT using your lower body, PRESS the weights overhead on an exhale.
Return on an inhale.
Up 2 counts, down 4.
Do 8 -15 reps.

II. PALMS FACE OUT PRESS

Using light weights, and NOT using your lower body, open the arms so that your elbows are next to the body, and the palms are facing out. Wrists are straight. PRESS overhead with an exhale, return on an inhale. Up 2 counts, down 4 counts.

III. PALMS IN PRESS

Using light weights, fold the elbows in to the front of the body, palms facing behind you, wrists straight. PRESS the weights overhead, keeping the shoulders down and stable. Up 2 counts, down 4 counts.

For a greater challenge, keep your hips stable and perform these 3 exercises on one leg. Repeat on the other leg. This engages the core and the stabilizers in the legs and hips. For a super-duper challenge, close your eyes!

TIPS!

- Keep your knees and elbows soft, not locked.
- Keep your shoulder girdle down throughout the movement.
- Are your wrists straight and your hands relaxed?

Now that you have determined your strength level on the different PRESS exercises, circle the PRESS in the FUNdamental WORKBOOK!

5 minutes of WARMUP

YOGA...SUN SALUTATION...3x's

SIT

PUSH

PULL

PRESS

Your choices are:

MEDICINE BALL TOSS UP
MEDICINE BALL SQUAT TOSS UP
MOUNTAIN CLIMBER
FLOOR JACKS
SIDE TO SIDE PRESS
HANDSTAND
PALMS FACING PRESS
PALMS FACE OUT PRESS
PALMS IN PRESS

❋ ❋ ❋ ❋ ❋ ❋ ❋ ❋ ❋ ❋ ❋

*Like puppies
and children,
rest when you are tired.
Eat less sugar.
Eat more fruits
and vegetables.*

THE CURL...FOR THE CORE

The CURL is a group of movements that involve all of the muscles of the trunk…your abdominals, your lower back, and *everything in between*, that help you rotate, balance and sit up.

THE CURL

The core moves in three basic directions:
1. Curling front to back
2. Twisting
3. Bending side to side

All three motions must be practiced to fully train the core.
Throughout the week, vary the motions so that you target the entire core.

1. *Curling forward and backward.* This movement is the most common one associated with the core. Anytime the body curls the chest towards the pelvis, or the pelvis toward the chest, the core muscles are in charge.

2. *Twisting.* Rotation of the core activates the oblique muscles and the lower back muscles. The movement rotates the torso and the upper body, by starting and stopping the action with the waist. All angles are important in this movement.

3. *Bending side to side.* This movement also curls the upper and lower bodies toward each other. We can do it on purpose with side crunches, or instinctively by bending to maintain balance.

In training the CURL, we will use
the CRUNCH,
a MEDICINE BALL,
and PILATES.

The CURL may feel odd at first. I find that most of my clients start at the beginner stage with these exercises, and as they are able to **focus on allowing the core to do most of the work,** *(rather than the legs, shoulders, arms, neck), they do fewer repetitions than they are used to. Once true awareness happens to the correct muscles, strength increases quickly, and then, so do the reps!*

THE
CURL

Let's establish great CURL form:

• Whether standing or lying down, the spine is neutral.

• Keep your head and neck in a natural line with the spine.

• Keep the muscles that aren't the core, as relaxed as possible:
arms, hands, feet, jaw, etc.

• Exhale on the hardest part of the movement, inhale on the return.

• Pay attention to which muscles get tired first.
These are usually the weaker ones of the group.

❈ ❈ ❈ ❈ ❈ ❈ ❈ ❈ ❈ ❈ ❈ ❈

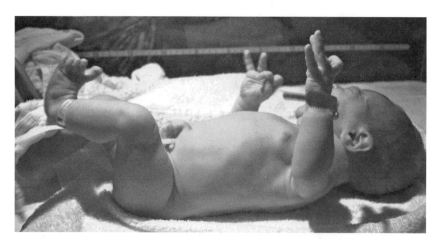

We have performed this motion since the day we were born…
it must be important!

❈ ❈ ❈ ❈ ❈ ❈ ❈ ❈ ❈ ❈ ❈ ❈

THE CRUNCH!

FORWARD AND BACK... **THE 123 CRUNCH**

This is the most famous CURL exercise, and when done properly, 8-15 repetitions is plenty! Remember that the CURL is about bringing the ribcage and the pelvis closer together. On your back, feeling your spine on the floor, bend your knees and support your head with your hands. On an exhale, CURL your chest toward your knees, and your knees toward your chin. You are peeling the upper body and tailbone off the floor, toward each other! Hold for three counts. Lower in one count, inhale.

1, 2, 3

Down

Start with 5 slow CRUNCHES, and increase as you feel it. Work up to 15 CRUNCHES!

THE
CURL

FORWARD AND BACK...**THE REVERSE CRUNCH**

This is a variation of the CRUNCH. On your back, arms at your sides, or overhead, peel your tailbone toward your chin. Lower slowly.
Use your core in this exercise! Keep the upper body and arms relaxed.
Allow your core to do the peeling. Exhale on the CURL.
For a greater challenge, place the arms overhead, on the floor.

*Be careful.
Roll only up to
the shoulder blades,
keeping the
neck relaxed and
the eyes facing up.*

Curl 2 counts

Release 2 counts

FORWARD AND BACK...**BACK EXTENSIONS!**

If we CURL forward, we must curl back!

1. Lie face down, and keep your hips and legs on the floor.
On an exhale, peel the upper body off the floor.
Peel 2 counts, hold 2 counts, down 2 counts.
Hands can be on the floor, by your ears, or straight out.

2. Reverse #1. Lie face down and keep your upper body on the floor.
Peel your straight legs, up to your hips, off the floor.
Up 2 counts, hold 2, down 2.

3. Extra credit! Combine 1 & 2, and peel the upper
and lower body toward each other, forming a "C" with the spine.
Up 2 counts, down 2.

TWISTING…**THE SEATED TWIST**

Seated, squiggle around until you find your sitbones…then find your tailbone.
Settle yourself between the sitbones and tailbone. Knees are bent with the feet lightly
on the floor. The core is strong. Lean slightly back with the abs crunched.
Using your waist (core), twist your shoulders, arms, hands, over to the right side, then left.
Be very aware of holding the correct position while you twist from side to side.
Touch 10-16 times alternating right and left.

BENDING SIDE TO SIDE…**SIDE CURLS!**

On your side, line up your body…feet, hips, elbow. Place the shoulder directly over
the elbow. Side CURL the lower waist, making a "C" and raising the hips off the floor.
Use your top hand if you need extra help. Exhale on the CURL up, inhale on the way down.

> *It is important to stretch your lower back after working the CURL. Fold yourself down, over slightly bent knees... let your neck relax. Feel your spine lengthening.*

Do you recognize the FORWARD BEND from YOGA?

ADAPTATIONS:

If the neck gets tired first:
Support your head gently with 1 or 2 hands, keeping the neck and head gently curving. Try pressing the head gently into the hands.

If lower back gets tired first:
Do the yoga warmup again, pausing at the cobra. When you return to the exercises, focus on CURLing the front of the core, not lifting or rotating the lower back. The lower back may get tired first...it is okay! The work for the CURL is being done!

If the hip flexors get tired:
Rest and stretch the pelvis up, lengthening the muscles and tendons between the knees and hips. Roll down feeling one vertebra touch the floor at a time. Resume the exercise!

If the arms, shoulders or hands get tired:
Close your eyes and feel the work being done in the center of your body. Relax everything else!

TIPS!

• As you CRUNCH, feel your torso peel, (not lift) the body away from the floor.
• Hold for a few seconds at the hardest part. Then release slowly.

THE MEDICINE BALL (MB)

Please try these exercises *without a medicine ball first*. It is very important to get the feel of the movement...starting and stopping the action with the waist...before adding weight.

FORWARD TO BACK...**LOW TO HIGH!**

Stand with the legs a little wider than the hips. With a flat back, bend over with arms between the legs. Squeezing the stomach muscles, on an exhale, lift/swing your arms overhead, just past vertical. Stop the motion with your stomach muscles! Curl forward, keeping the arms by your ears, and the back flat, until the bottom of the exercise. Do 5 repetitions to start. When you can do 8-10, add a 2-4 lb. medicine ball.

TWISTING...**180° +**

Stand with feet just wider than the shoulders. Pretend you are six years old and *using your waist*, rotate the torso from side to side. The arms/feet/medicine ball, follow the action of the waist. Start and stop the movement with the waist!

MORE TWISTING!

DIAGONAL CORE ROTATION... **THE "X"**

Pretend you are a warrior in *Star Wars,* using a light saber! Cut the sky with a giant "X", starting and stopping the action with the core!

Start with feet just wider than the hips. Knees are soft and back stays flat! Bend and twist the torso to the back wall, keeping the chest lifted and the back flat. Rotate the waist at a diagonal, up and across, to the other side. Let the waist start and stop this movement.

BENDING SIDE TO SIDE!... **TICK-TOCK!**

Standing with feet together, knees soft, and arms overhead, bend at the waist, stretching your side. On an exhale, use the waist muscles to stand upright. Repeat on the other side. Tick-tock slowly, concentrating on allowing the core to do the work. Add a MB as you get stronger.

It is sometimes easier to feel this exercise with your eyes closed!

❋ ❋ ❋ ❋ ❋ ❋ ❋ ❋ ❋ ❋ ❋ ❋

TIPS!

- *Feel the work happening in your core without the ball.*
  - *Is you center "starting and stopping" the motion?*
  - *Are your arms, and the MB, extensions of your core?*

❋ ❋ ❋ ❋ ❋ ❋ ❋ ❋ ❋ ❋ ❋ ❋

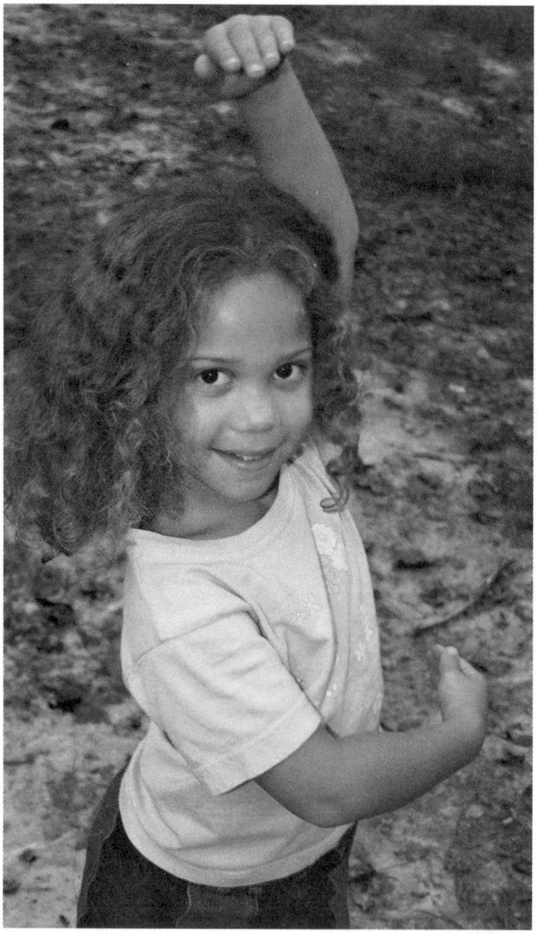

Dance every day...
keep the blues away.

PILATES

Pilates is a style of movement, designed by Josef Pilates, that brings out the dancer in us all. These movements focus on building core strength, while lengthening the not-so-kid-anymore muscles. As you practice these Pilates movements, think like a ballerina, point your toes, go slow, bringing your attention and efforts to your center.

In all of these exercises, your own body weight and resistance are your guides to where to start, and when to increase strength. These movements look easier than they are, so be patient, trust yourself, and work with great form. Rest often, stretch, and resume. Do only as many repetitions as you can while maintaining great form. If you get tired and lose your form, it is time to rest!

Let's establish great PILATES form…

- On your back, close your eyes and feel each vertebra touching the floor. Roll your head, neck and shoulders up, unpeeling them from the ground…always feeling your spine touching the floor. Lower them back down. Tuck your pelvis under slightly (pelvic tilt), feeling your lower spine connect with the floor. Release. Both of these actions are starting in your center or abdomen. Try it again, and be sure to initiate the action from your center.

- Keeping the spine neutral (or natural), exhale your stomach muscles in toward your spine. Hold this firm. This is your *strong center!*

> *The extending of the legs or arms adds weight to the action at the core. Moving the limbs and keeping the core strong and firm is the basis for the CURL Pilates work. Enjoy!*

THE
CURL

Let's CURL with PILATES!

FORWARD AND BACK...**PILATES SINGLE LEG STRETCH!**

On your back, with your core pressed into the floor, and your head and shoulders peeled off the floor, pull your right leg in toward your chest.
Feel your strong center as you hold that stretch. Keeping your toes pointed and your legs long, switch legs...bring the left knee in.

Exhale each time you switch legs,
or when the knee is closest to the chest.
Start with 10 repetitions,
(each knee in counts as 1).
Work toward 20, then 30.
Keep this slow and controlled,
but keep it moving!

Remember, the action at the core is happening as you switch the legs back and forth.
By keeping the *strong center,* you are challenging the whole core!

FORWARD AND BACK...**THE SWIMMER!**

Now for the opposite direction!
Lie face down, keeping your hips and pelvis on the floor. Keeping a *strong center,*
point your toes, straighten your arms and legs, and gently kick the air up and down.
Be as long as you can be–reach forward, point backward, and look at your fingertips.
By arching up slightly and moving the limbs, your are challenging the entire lower back,
upper back, buns, and core. Congratulations!

Start swimming for 10 seconds,
moving your opposite arm
and leg. Rest. Repeat.
Do it three times.
Work up to 20 seconds,
and then 30 seconds.

TWISTING...**THE PILATES BICYCLE!**

Using the same starting form as the SINGLE LEG STRETCH, lightly support your head
with your hands, shoulders relaxed. CURL both shoulders toward your left knee,
and switch. Keep the *strong center*, with your belly button pressed toward the floor.
The eyes are looking at your knees, with the neck naturally curling with the spine.
Count 10 repetitions (one count per leg). Rest. Repeat 2 more times.
Work up to 20 reps, then 30!

✻ ✻ ✻ ✻ ✻ ✻ ✻ ✻ ✻ ✻ ✻ ✻ ✻

TIPS!

• *Don't pull on your head with your arms.*
• *Keep your fingertips around your ears.*

✻ ✻ ✻ ✻ ✻ ✻ ✻ ✻ ✻ ✻ ✻ ✻ ✻

*SIDE TO SIDE...***BALLET EXTENSIONS!**

On your side, line up your hand, hips, legs, and toes. Remember to keep that shoulder girdle shrugged down and strong.

Spread your fingers out, and with your waist, CURL your lower ribcage toward your hip bone. This crunch raises the body, and allows you to extend and lengthen your opposite side. Raise up 4 counts, then lower 4 counts. Start with 4 of these. Rest. Switch sides. Work up to 6 per side...then 8!

Exhale on the way up...inhale on the way down.
Do you feel like a dancer now?

Now we are ready to circle the CURL
in the FUNdamental WORKBOOK!

5 minutes of WARMUP

YOGA...SUN SALUTATION...3 x's

SIT

PUSH

PULL

PRESS

CURL

Your choices are:

CRUNCH   123 CRUNCH
             REVERSE CRUNCH
             BACK EXTENSIONS
             SEATED TWIST
             SIDE CURLS

> *Remember to work all three motions of the CURL: forward & back, twisting, and side to side, throughout the week.*

MEDICINE   LO TO HI
BALL   180° +
             THE "X"
             TICK-TOCK

PILATES   SINGLE LEG STRETCH
             SWIMMER
             BICYCLE
             BALLET EXTENSIONS

❋ ❋ ❋ ❋ ❋ ❋ ❋ ❋ ❋ ❋ ❋ ❋

Diversity, balance,
and laughter are the keys
to a great workout!

TOTAL BODY MOVEMENTS

Total Body Movements are exercises that mimic everyday life.
The TBM's are designed to build strength in muscles
throughout a variety of planes of motion, or multidimensionally,
just like we move every day…only deeper!
These exercises help build cardio (if you do them quickly),
balance (if you do them slowly), and coordination (no matter what)!

TOTAL BODY MOVEMENTS

We will use exercises from the SIT, PUSH, PULL, PRESS, and CURL, and combine them, creating new movements that let us practice and strengthen the firing patterns used in normal life. Some of the most fit people I know get injured when they bend over to pick up their keys, or when they are playing on the floor with their grandchildren. Here's how we can train those movements!

THE MATRIX

When you bend over to tie your shoe, or pick up your keys, you have performed a part of the Matrix. By combining the SIT, CURL, and PRESS, we are strengthening the firing patterns of the lower back, the rear end, and the legs...areas with a tendency for injury. Try this series without weights, and as you get comfortable, add 3-5 lbs. per hand, or a 4-6 lb medicine ball.

MATRIX I.

Start with feet together, arms by your side.
take a medium step forward, mostly heel,
and with a flat back and strong abs, bend the
body over the knee (as if you were picking up keys).
With the forward foot, push back to standing,
and PRESS the arms overhead.
Repeat 8 X's on the right leg. Switch legs.
When this feels strong, alternate the legs.

MATRIX II.

Feet together, step directly to the right,
keeping toes, knees and hips forward.
The knee stays over the foot! With a flat back
and strong abs, bend over the right knee.
Return the feet together, PRESS arms overhead.
Repeat 8 X's on the right side, then left.
When this feels strong, try alternating, left and right.

MATRIX III.

Feet together, step back at a 45° angle,
And with a flat back and strong abs,
bend over the outside knee.
Return to standing and PRESS overhead.
Repeat 8 X's on the right. Then left.
Alternate sides when you feel ready!

You can do each Matrix segment separately, or you can combine the three parts
for a challenging, multidirectional TBM.

Matrix I. ... Alternating 8-16 X's
Matrix II. ... Alternating 8-16 X's
Matrix III. ... Alternating 8-16 X's

Add light weights and increase the speed to increase the challenge.
Your exertion level is between 6-8, depending on what you want.

*Be aware! The Matrix is slightly deceptive. Start with a few reps
per side, and gradually increase. The rear end and leg muscles are
getting fatigued without you knowing it...until the next day!
Enjoy tapping into muscles that we use on
a daily basis, but rarely spend time strengthening.*

THE SQUAT PRESS

This exercise combines the SIT and the PRESS. Use light weights and increase as you grow stronger. Allow yourself to use your legs to PRESS the arms overhead. Think of it being one big motion.

Do 8-15 repetitions at an exertion level of 6-8.

Notice that you have strengthened your legs, rear end, core, and shoulder girdle... and heart and lungs!

Squat

Press!

THE YOGA AIRPLANE

This is my favorite, because it makes me feel like a ballerina.
This motion combines the CURL and YOGA, with balance and focus.
Start with two or three reps on each side, and increase to 6 as your core
and stabilizers get strong! Practice with and without shoes.
Exertion level 4-5.

Balance on your left leg. Lift your right leg and CURL around it. Hold for 4 counts.

Straighten your body up into a tall "T". Your right leg is pointed strong behind you, with your buns squeezed tight, and your back slightly arched. Hold for 4 counts.

In one strong, slow motion, act as a see-saw and lower the body toward parallel to the floor. Keep the body strong and straight, and only lower as far as the leg can come up, or the chest can go down.
Hold for 4 counts.

CURL or tuck back into the starting position and repeat 2-6 times on each side.

This TBM uses a lot of core/trunk. If you feel tight, stretch with the YOGA Poses—Forward Bend and Back Bend—to release.

THE BURPEE!

This TBM uses mainly the SIT and the PUSH, but the core will get its fair share of work too! Oh, don't forget the heart and lungs!

Stand.
Smile.

Squat to the floor, putting both hands on the floor.

Keeping the shoulder girdle shrugged toward the waist, and the weight on the hands, straighten the right leg, then left leg back to a PLANK.

Return legs, right, then left, to the squat.

Stand.

That is one BURPEE! Do 5, increase to 10 with practice.
Start slowly, and as your heart and body condition, increase the speed.

BURPEE EXTRA!

Once you have mastered the BURPEE, challenge yourself with this!

Squat   Jump to plank   Push up   Stand. Smile.

This TBM is the BURPEE with both legs moving back simultaneously,
plus an added knee PUSHUP (or regular PUSHUP), from the PLANK position.
So...Stand. Squat. Jump feet out to plank. Push up. Jump feet to squat. Stand.
Extra credit is given for jumping to the final standing position.
Start with 5, and increase to 10x. Have fun!

The TBM fits into the FUNdamental Workout after the PUSH, PULL, PRESS, CURL, SIT circuit.
As a combination drill, it pulls the workout together, reminding the body how it truly works
as one fluid unit. The TBM also elevates the heart rate, intensifying the circuit and preparing
you for a two-minute cardio training interval.

Pick one TMB, do it for one minute, or 5-10 reps.

For extra cardio training, the workout has a two-minute CARDIO interval done after the TBM,
at an exertion level of 6, 7, or 8.
Add the CARDIO interval when you are ready, and enjoy the buzz!

CARDIO

The term CARDIO implies moving your body hard or fast enough, so that on a scale from 1-10, you feel yourself working at a 6, 7, or 8. (9 and 10 are optional levels). You may breathe heavier, you may sweat, you may feel an exuberant rush of pure happiness as your body responds to the challenge.

Watch a playground. Kids do it effortlessly. That is our goal.

For 2 minutes, (or one early Beatles' tune), try these feel-like-a kid-again intervals:

• SKIP in place, or SKIP around the house. If you have forgotten how…ask an expert!

• JUMP ROPE, or pretend to. Count how many jumps it takes to fill 2 minutes. See if you can get more jumps each time you try this!

• STEP UP/DOWN, on a 4-8" platform or bench. This is a moving SIT!

• WALK briskly.

• JOG lightly.

• JUMPING JACKS

…or any 2 minute combination of the above choices.
Let yourself feel wonderfully young!

Now add the TMB and CARDIO to the FUNdamental Workout.
Circle one of each and add them to your circuit.
Write the number of repetitions or seconds in the blank.
Your *FUNdamental Fitness* Workout is complete!

5 minutes of WARMUP

YOGA...SUN SALUTATION...3 x's

SIT

PUSH

PULL

PRESS

CURL

TBM
Your choices are:

MATRIX
SQUAT PRESS
YOGA AIRPLANE
BURPEE
BURPEE EXTRA!

CARDIO
Your choices are:

SKIP
JUMP ROPE
STEP UP/DOWN
WALK BRISKLY
JOG LIGHTLY
JUMPING JACKS

YOGA 3 X'S FOR COOLDOWN!

❋ ❋ ❋ ❋ ❋ ❋ ❋ ❋ ❋ ❋ ❋

PART FOUR

THE FUNdamental FITNESS WORKBOOK

Now it is up to you.
You have the tools, the concept, the references for form,
and the pictures of children for inspiration.
Find your goal. Match it with your desire. Take action.

On the next page is a sample *FUNdamental Fitness* Workout to get you started.
Use it to get a flow going and to signal your creativity.
Remember that these are just a few of the hundreds of ways to move, challenge,
and strengthen the body. Keep your mind open, enjoy, and experiment!
Circle your choices. Fill in the blank the number of repetitions
and the amount of weight or resistance used for that exercise.
Rest 30 seconds between movements.
If needed, turn to the page number to see details of the exercise.
Keep the circuit flowing. Slow down at the Yoga.

Think like a kid again!
Move like a kid again!
Feel like a kid again!

❉ ❉ ❉ ❉ ❉ ❉ ❉ ❉ ❉ ❉ ❉ ❉

Enjoy FUNdamental Fitness *as often as you want to.*
Every other day is wonderful,
Remember...the body responds to consistency,
intensity, and variety!

FUNdamental Fitness WORKOUT

WARMUP

YOGA - 3x's PG. 25 - 29

_____30 seconds_____ SIT

_____10x on knees_____ PUSH

_____15x_____ PULL

_____15x w/4lb. MB_____ PRESS

_____10x per side_____ CURL

_____8x I, II_____ TBM

_____2 minutes_____ CARDIO

YOGA - 3x's PG. 25 - 29

TODAY IS ____August 27_____

I DID THE CIRCUIT ___2___ TIMES

IT TOOK ME __30__ MINUTES

I FEEL _____energized_____!

SIT
WALL SQUAT
MOVING SQUAT
SWISS BALL SQUAT
BACKWARD LUNGE
FORWARD LUNGE
BACK & FORWARD LUNGE
SIT AND LUNGE
SQUAT JUMP
ON YOUR MARK!
} PG. 35 - 47

PUSH
PUSH UP
PUSH UP W/POWER
PLANK
MOVING PLANK
SWISS BALL WALKOUTS
GI JOE (THE CRAWL)
MEDICINE BALL TOSS
YOGA PUSHUPS
} PG. 49 - 61

PULL
WATER SKIER
PIZZA PAN
CROSS COUNTRY SKIER
ONE ARM ROW
TWO ARM ROW
FLIES
SKI POLING
BAR SQUAT PULLUP
BAR ANGLE PULL
BAR JUMP PULLUP
} PG. 63 - 73

PRESS
MEDICINE BALL TOSS UP
MB SQUAT & TOSS UP
MOUNTAIN CLIMBER
FLOOR JACKS
SIDE TO SIDE PRESS
HANDSTAND
PALMS FACING PRESS
PALMS FACE OUT PRESS
PALMS IN PRESS
} PG. 75 - 85

CURL
123 CRUNCH
REVERSE CRUNCH
BACK EXTENSIONS
SEATED TWIST
SIDE CURLS
MEDICINE BALL LO TO HI
180° +
THE "X"
TICK-TOCK
SINGLE LEG STRETCH
SWIMMER
BICYCLE
BALLET EXTENSIONS
} PG. 87 - 103

TBM
MATRIX I, II, III
SQUAT PRESS
YOGA AIRPLANE
BURPEE!
BURPEE EXTRA!
} PG. 105 - 111

CARDIO
SKIP
JUMP ROPE
STEP UP/DOWN
WALK BRISKLY
JOG LIGHTLY
JUMPING JACKS
} PG. 112

FUNdamental Fitness WORKOUT

WARMUP

YOGA - 3x's PG. 25 - 29

_____ SIT

_____ PUSH

_____ PULL

_____ PRESS

_____ CURL

_____ TBM

_____ CARDIO

YOGA - 3x's PG. 25 - 29

TODAY IS _____

I DID THE CIRCUIT _____ TIMES

IT TOOK ME _____ MINUTES

I FEEL _____!

SIT
WALL SQUAT
MOVING SQUAT
SWISS BALL SQUAT
BACKWARD LUNGE
FORWARD LUNGE
BACK & FORWARD LUNGE
SIT AND LUNGE
SQUAT JUMP
ON YOUR MARK!
} PG. 35 - 47

PUSH
PUSH UP
PUSH UP W/POWER
PLANK
MOVING PLANK
SWISS BALL WALKOUTS
GI JOE (THE CRAWL)
MEDICINE BALL TOSS
YOGA PUSHUPS
} PG. 49 - 61

PULL
WATER SKIER
PIZZA PAN
CROSS COUNTRY SKIER
ONE ARM ROW
TWO ARM ROW
FLIES
SKI POLING
BAR SQUAT PULLUP
BAR ANGLE PULL
BAR JUMP PULLUP
} PG. 63 - 73

PRESS
MEDICINE BALL TOSS UP
MB SQUAT & TOSS UP
MOUNTAIN CLIMBER
FLOOR JACKS
SIDE TO SIDE PRESS
HANDSTAND
PALMS FACING PRESS
PALMS FACE OUT PRESS
PALMS IN PRESS
} PG. 75 - 85

CURL
123 CRUNCH
REVERSE CRUNCH
BACK EXTENSIONS
SEATED TWIST
SIDE CURLS
MEDICINE BALL LO TO HI
180° +
THE "X"
TICK-TOCK
SINGLE LEG STRETCH
SWIMMER
BICYCLE
BALLET EXTENSIONS
} PG. 87 - 103

TBM
MATRIX I, II, III
SQUAT PRESS
YOGA AIRPLANE
BURPEE!
BURPEE EXTRA!
} PG. 105 - 111

CARDIO
SKIP
JUMP ROPE
STEP UP/DOWN
WALK BRISKLY
JOG LIGHTLY
JUMPING JACKS
} PG. 112

FUNdamental Fitness WORKOUT

WARMUP

YOGA - 3x's PG. 25 - 29

_____ SIT

_____ PUSH

_____ PULL

_____ PRESS

_____ CURL

_____ TBM

_____ CARDIO

YOGA - 3x's PG. 25 - 29

TODAY IS _____

I DID THE CIRCUIT _____ TIMES

IT TOOK ME _____ MINUTES

I FEEL _____!

SIT
WALL SQUAT
MOVING SQUAT
SWISS BALL SQUAT
BACKWARD LUNGE
FORWARD LUNGE
BACK & FORWARD LUNGE
SIT AND LUNGE
SQUAT JUMP
ON YOUR MARK!
} PG. 35 - 47

PUSH
PUSH UP
PUSH UP W/POWER
PLANK
MOVING PLANK
SWISS BALL WALKOUTS
GI JOE (THE CRAWL)
MEDICINE BALL TOSS
YOGA PUSHUPS
} PG. 49 - 61

PULL
WATER SKIER
PIZZA PAN
CROSS COUNTRY SKIER
ONE ARM ROW
TWO ARM ROW
FLIES
SKI POLING
BAR SQUAT PULLUP
BAR ANGLE PULL
BAR JUMP PULLUP
} PG. 63 - 73

PRESS
MEDICINE BALL TOSS UP
MB SQUAT & TOSS UP
MOUNTAIN CLIMBER
FLOOR JACKS
SIDE TO SIDE PRESS
HANDSTAND
PALMS FACING PRESS
PALMS FACE OUT PRESS
PALMS IN PRESS
} PG. 75 - 85

CURL
123 CRUNCH
REVERSE CRUNCH
BACK EXTENSIONS
SEATED TWIST
SIDE CURLS
MEDICINE BALL LO TO HI
180° +
THE "X"
TICK-TOCK
SINGLE LEG STRETCH
SWIMMER
BICYCLE
BALLET EXTENSIONS
} PG. 87 - 103

TBM
MATRIX I, II, III
SQUAT PRESS
YOGA AIRPLANE
BURPEE!
BURPEE EXTRA!
} PG. 105 - 111

CARDIO
SKIP
JUMP ROPE
STEP UP/DOWN
WALK BRISKLY
JOG LIGHTLY
JUMPING JACKS
} PG. 112

FUNdamental Fitness WORKOUT

WARMUP

YOGA - 3x's PG. 25 - 29

_____ SIT

_____ PUSH

_____ PULL

_____ PRESS

_____ CURL

_____ TBM

_____ CARDIO

YOGA - 3x's PG. 25 - 29

TODAY IS _____

I DID THE CIRCUIT _____ TIMES

IT TOOK ME _____ MINUTES

I FEEL _____!

SIT
WALL SQUAT
MOVING SQUAT
SWISS BALL SQUAT
BACKWARD LUNGE
FORWARD LUNGE
BACK & FORWARD LUNGE
SIT AND LUNGE
SQUAT JUMP
ON YOUR MARK!
} PG. 35 - 47

PUSH
PUSH UP
PUSH UP W/POWER
PLANK
MOVING PLANK
SWISS BALL WALKOUTS
GI JOE (THE CRAWL)
MEDICINE BALL TOSS
YOGA PUSHUPS
} PG. 49 - 61

PULL
WATER SKIER
PIZZA PAN
CROSS COUNTRY SKIER
ONE ARM ROW
TWO ARM ROW
FLIES
SKI POLING
BAR SQUAT PULLUP
BAR ANGLE PULL
BAR JUMP PULLUP
} PG. 63 - 73

PRESS
MEDICINE BALL TOSS UP
MB SQUAT & TOSS UP
MOUNTAIN CLIMBER
FLOOR JACKS
SIDE TO SIDE PRESS
HANDSTAND
PALMS FACING PRESS
PALMS FACE OUT PRESS
PALMS IN PRESS
} PG. 75 - 85

CURL
123 CRUNCH
REVERSE CRUNCH
BACK EXTENSIONS
SEATED TWIST
SIDE CURLS
MEDICINE BALL LO TO HI
$180° +$
THE "X"
TICK-TOCK
SINGLE LEG STRETCH
SWIMMER
BICYCLE
BALLET EXTENSIONS
} PG. 87 - 103

TBM
MATRIX I, II, III
SQUAT PRESS
YOGA AIRPLANE
BURPEE!
BURPEE EXTRA!
} PG. 105 - 111

CARDIO
SKIP
JUMP ROPE
STEP UP/DOWN
WALK BRISKLY
JOG LIGHTLY
JUMPING JACKS
} PG. 112

FUNdamental Fitness WORKOUT

WARMUP

YOGA - 3x's PG. 25 - 29

_____ SIT

_____ PUSH

_____ PULL

_____ PRESS

_____ CURL

_____ TBM

_____ CARDIO

YOGA - 3x's PG. 25 - 29

TODAY IS _____

I DID THE CIRCUIT _____ TIMES

IT TOOK ME _____ MINUTES

I FEEL _____!

SIT
WALL SQUAT
MOVING SQUAT
SWISS BALL SQUAT
BACKWARD LUNGE
FORWARD LUNGE
BACK & FORWARD LUNGE
SIT AND LUNGE
SQUAT JUMP
ON YOUR MARK!
} PG. 35 - 47

PUSH
PUSH UP
PUSH UP W/POWER
PLANK
MOVING PLANK
SWISS BALL WALKOUTS
GI JOE (THE CRAWL)
MEDICINE BALL TOSS
YOGA PUSHUPS
} PG. 49 - 61

PULL
WATER SKIER
PIZZA PAN
CROSS COUNTRY SKIER
ONE ARM ROW
TWO ARM ROW
FLIES
SKI POLING
BAR SQUAT PULLUP
BAR ANGLE PULL
BAR JUMP PULLUP
} PG. 63 - 73

PRESS
MEDICINE BALL TOSS UP
MB SQUAT & TOSS UP
MOUNTAIN CLIMBER
FLOOR JACKS
SIDE TO SIDE PRESS
HANDSTAND
PALMS FACING PRESS
PALMS FACE OUT PRESS
PALMS IN PRESS
} PG. 75 - 85

CURL
123 CRUNCH
REVERSE CRUNCH
BACK EXTENSIONS
SEATED TWIST
SIDE CURLS
MEDICINE BALL LO TO HI
180° +
THE "X"
TICK-TOCK
SINGLE LEG STRETCH
SWIMMER
BICYCLE
BALLET EXTENSIONS
} PG. 87 - 103

TBM
MATRIX I, II, III
SQUAT PRESS
YOGA AIRPLANE
BURPEE!
BURPEE EXTRA!
} PG. 105 - 111

CARDIO
SKIP
JUMP ROPE
STEP UP/DOWN
WALK BRISKLY
JOG LIGHTLY
JUMPING JACKS
} PG. 112

FUNdamental Fitness WORKOUT

WARMUP

YOGA - 3x's PG. 25 - 29

_____ SIT

_____ PUSH

_____ PULL

_____ PRESS

_____ CURL

_____ TBM

_____ CARDIO

YOGA - 3x's PG. 25 - 29

TODAY IS _____

I DID THE CIRCUIT _____ TIMES

IT TOOK ME _____ MINUTES

I FEEL _____!

SIT
WALL SQUAT
MOVING SQUAT
SWISS BALL SQUAT
BACKWARD LUNGE
FORWARD LUNGE
BACK & FORWARD LUNGE
SIT AND LUNGE
SQUAT JUMP
ON YOUR MARK!
} PG. 35 - 47

PUSH
PUSH UP
PUSH UP W/POWER
PLANK
MOVING PLANK
SWISS BALL WALKOUTS
GI JOE (THE CRAWL)
MEDICINE BALL TOSS
YOGA PUSHUPS
} PG. 49 - 61

PULL
WATER SKIER
PIZZA PAN
CROSS COUNTRY SKIER
ONE ARM ROW
TWO ARM ROW
FLIES
SKI POLING
BAR SQUAT PULLUP
BAR ANGLE PULL
BAR JUMP PULLUP
} PG. 63 - 73

PRESS
MEDICINE BALL TOSS UP
MB SQUAT & TOSS UP
MOUNTAIN CLIMBER
FLOOR JACKS
SIDE TO SIDE PRESS
HANDSTAND
PALMS FACING PRESS
PALMS FACE OUT PRESS
PALMS IN PRESS
} PG. 75 - 85

CURL
123 CRUNCH
REVERSE CRUNCH
BACK EXTENSIONS
SEATED TWIST
SIDE CURLS
MEDICINE BALL LO TO HI
180° +
THE "X"
TICK-TOCK
SINGLE LEG STRETCH
SWIMMER
BICYCLE
BALLET EXTENSIONS
} PG. 87 - 103

TBM
MATRIX I, II, III
SQUAT PRESS
YOGA AIRPLANE
BURPEE!
BURPEE EXTRA!
} PG. 105 - 111

CARDIO
SKIP
JUMP ROPE
STEP UP/DOWN
WALK BRISKLY
JOG LIGHTLY
JUMPING JACKS
} PG. 112

FUNdamental Fitness WORKOUT

WARMUP

YOGA - 3x's PG. 25 - 29

_____ SIT

_____ PUSH

_____ PULL

_____ PRESS

_____ CURL

_____ TBM

_____ CARDIO

YOGA - 3x's PG. 25 - 29

TODAY IS _____

I DID THE CIRCUIT _____ TIMES

IT TOOK ME _____ MINUTES

I FEEL _____!

SIT
WALL SQUAT
MOVING SQUAT
SWISS BALL SQUAT
BACKWARD LUNGE
FORWARD LUNGE
BACK & FORWARD LUNGE
SIT AND LUNGE
SQUAT JUMP
ON YOUR MARK!
PG. 35 - 47

PUSH
PUSH UP
PUSH UP W/POWER
PLANK
MOVING PLANK
SWISS BALL WALKOUTS
GI JOE (THE CRAWL)
MEDICINE BALL TOSS
YOGA PUSHUPS
PG. 49 - 61

PULL
WATER SKIER
PIZZA PAN
CROSS COUNTRY SKIER
ONE ARM ROW
TWO ARM ROW
FLIES
SKI POLING
BAR SQUAT PULLUP
BAR ANGLE PULL
BAR JUMP PULLUP
PG. 63 - 73

PRESS
MEDICINE BALL TOSS UP
MB SQUAT & TOSS UP
MOUNTAIN CLIMBER
FLOOR JACKS
SIDE TO SIDE PRESS
HANDSTAND
PALMS FACING PRESS
PALMS FACE OUT PRESS
PALMS IN PRESS
PG. 75 - 85

CURL
123 CRUNCH
REVERSE CRUNCH
BACK EXTENSIONS
SEATED TWIST
SIDE CURLS
MEDICINE BALL LO TO HI
180° +
THE "X"
TICK-TOCK
SINGLE LEG STRETCH
SWIMMER
BICYCLE
BALLET EXTENSIONS
PG. 87 - 103

TBM
MATRIX I, II, III
SQUAT PRESS
YOGA AIRPLANE
BURPEE!
BURPEE EXTRA!
PG. 105 - 111

CARDIO
SKIP
JUMP ROPE
STEP UP/DOWN
WALK BRISKLY
JOG LIGHTLY
JUMPING JACKS
PG. 112

FUNdamental Fitness WORKOUT

WARMUP

YOGA - 3x's PG. 25 - 29

_____ SIT

_____ PUSH

_____ PULL

_____ PRESS

_____ CURL

_____ TBM

_____ CARDIO

YOGA - 3x's PG. 25 - 29

TODAY IS _____

I DID THE CIRCUIT _____ TIMES

IT TOOK ME _____ MINUTES

I FEEL _____ !

SIT
WALL SQUAT
MOVING SQUAT
SWISS BALL SQUAT
BACKWARD LUNGE
FORWARD LUNGE
BACK & FORWARD LUNGE
SIT AND LUNGE
SQUAT JUMP
ON YOUR MARK!
} PG. 35 - 47

PUSH
PUSH UP
PUSH UP W/POWER
PLANK
MOVING PLANK
SWISS BALL WALKOUTS
GI JOE (THE CRAWL)
MEDICINE BALL TOSS
YOGA PUSHUPS
} PG. 49 - 61

PULL
WATER SKIER
PIZZA PAN
CROSS COUNTRY SKIER
ONE ARM ROW
TWO ARM ROW
FLIES
SKI POLING
BAR SQUAT PULLUP
BAR ANGLE PULL
BAR JUMP PULLUP
} PG. 63 - 73

PRESS
MEDICINE BALL TOSS UP
MB SQUAT & TOSS UP
MOUNTAIN CLIMBER
FLOOR JACKS
SIDE TO SIDE PRESS
HANDSTAND
PALMS FACING PRESS
PALMS FACE OUT PRESS
PALMS IN PRESS
} PG. 75 - 85

CURL
123 CRUNCH
REVERSE CRUNCH
BACK EXTENSIONS
SEATED TWIST
SIDE CURLS
MEDICINE BALL LO TO HI
180° +
THE "X"
TICK-TOCK
SINGLE LEG STRETCH
SWIMMER
BICYCLE
BALLET EXTENSIONS
} PG. 87 - 103

TBM
MATRIX I, II, III
SQUAT PRESS
YOGA AIRPLANE
BURPEE!
BURPEE EXTRA!
} PG. 105 - 111

CARDIO
SKIP
JUMP ROPE
STEP UP/DOWN
WALK BRISKLY
JOG LIGHTLY
JUMPING JACKS
} PG. 112

FUNdamental Fitness WORKOUT

WARMUP

YOGA - 3x's PG. 25 - 29

_____ SIT

_____ PUSH

_____ PULL

_____ PRESS

_____ CURL

_____ TBM

_____ CARDIO

YOGA - 3x's PG. 25 - 29

TODAY IS _____

I DID THE CIRCUIT _____ TIMES

IT TOOK ME _____ MINUTES

I FEEL _____!

SIT
WALL SQUAT
MOVING SQUAT
SWISS BALL SQUAT
BACKWARD LUNGE
FORWARD LUNGE
BACK & FORWARD LUNGE
SIT AND LUNGE
SQUAT JUMP
ON YOUR MARK!
} PG. 35 - 47

PUSH
PUSH UP
PUSH UP W/POWER
PLANK
MOVING PLANK
SWISS BALL WALKOUTS
GI JOE (THE CRAWL)
MEDICINE BALL TOSS
YOGA PUSHUPS
} PG. 49 - 61

PULL
WATER SKIER
PIZZA PAN
CROSS COUNTRY SKIER
ONE ARM ROW
TWO ARM ROW
FLIES
SKI POLING
BAR SQUAT PULLUP
BAR ANGLE PULL
BAR JUMP PULLUP
} PG. 63 - 73

PRESS
MEDICINE BALL TOSS UP
MB SQUAT & TOSS UP
MOUNTAIN CLIMBER
FLOOR JACKS
SIDE TO SIDE PRESS
HANDSTAND
PALMS FACING PRESS
PALMS FACE OUT PRESS
PALMS IN PRESS
} PG. 75 - 85

CURL
123 CRUNCH
REVERSE CRUNCH
BACK EXTENSIONS
SEATED TWIST
SIDE CURLS
MEDICINE BALL LO TO HI
180° +
THE "X"
TICK-TOCK
SINGLE LEG STRETCH
SWIMMER
BICYCLE
BALLET EXTENSIONS
} PG. 87 - 103

TBM
MATRIX I, II, III
SQUAT PRESS
YOGA AIRPLANE
BURPEE!
BURPEE EXTRA!
} PG. 105 - 111

CARDIO
SKIP
JUMP ROPE
STEP UP/DOWN
WALK BRISKLY
JOG LIGHTLY
JUMPING JACKS
} PG. 112

FUNdamental Fitness WORKOUT

WARMUP

YOGA - 3x's PG. 25 - 29

_____ SIT

_____ PUSH

_____ PULL

_____ PRESS

_____ CURL

_____ TBM

_____ CARDIO

YOGA - 3x's PG. 25 - 29

TODAY IS _____

I DID THE CIRCUIT _____ TIMES

IT TOOK ME _____ MINUTES

I FEEL _____!

SIT
WALL SQUAT
MOVING SQUAT
SWISS BALL SQUAT
BACKWARD LUNGE
FORWARD LUNGE
BACK & FORWARD LUNGE
SIT AND LUNGE
SQUAT JUMP
ON YOUR MARK!
} PG. 35 - 47

PUSH
PUSH UP
PUSH UP W/POWER
PLANK
MOVING PLANK
SWISS BALL WALKOUTS
GI JOE (THE CRAWL)
MEDICINE BALL TOSS
YOGA PUSHUPS
} PG. 49 - 61

PULL
WATER SKIER
PIZZA PAN
CROSS COUNTRY SKIER
ONE ARM ROW
TWO ARM ROW
FLIES
SKI POLING
BAR SQUAT PULLUP
BAR ANGLE PULL
BAR JUMP PULLUP
} PG. 63 - 73

PRESS
MEDICINE BALL TOSS UP
MB SQUAT & TOSS UP
MOUNTAIN CLIMBER
FLOOR JACKS
SIDE TO SIDE PRESS
HANDSTAND
PALMS FACING PRESS
PALMS FACE OUT PRESS
PALMS IN PRESS
} PG. 75 - 85

CURL
123 CRUNCH
REVERSE CRUNCH
BACK EXTENSIONS
SEATED TWIST
SIDE CURLS
MEDICINE BALL LO TO HI
180° +
THE "X"
TICK-TOCK
SINGLE LEG STRETCH
SWIMMER
BICYCLE
BALLET EXTENSIONS
} PG. 87 - 103

TBM
MATRIX I, II, III
SQUAT PRESS
YOGA AIRPLANE
BURPEE!
BURPEE EXTRA!
} PG. 105 - 111

CARDIO
SKIP
JUMP ROPE
STEP UP/DOWN
WALK BRISKLY
JOG LIGHTLY
JUMPING JACKS
} PG. 112

FUNdamental Fitness WORKOUT

WARMUP

YOGA - 3x's PG. 25 - 29

_____ SIT

_____ PUSH

_____ PULL

_____ PRESS

_____ CURL

_____ TBM

_____ CARDIO

YOGA - 3x's PG. 25 - 29

TODAY IS _____

I DID THE CIRCUIT _____ TIMES

IT TOOK ME _____ MINUTES

I FEEL _____!

SIT
WALL SQUAT
MOVING SQUAT
SWISS BALL SQUAT
BACKWARD LUNGE   } PG. 35 - 47
FORWARD LUNGE
BACK & FORWARD LUNGE
SIT AND LUNGE
SQUAT JUMP
ON YOUR MARK!

PUSH
PUSH UP
PUSH UP W/POWER
PLANK
MOVING PLANK   } PG. 49 - 61
SWISS BALL WALKOUTS
GI JOE (THE CRAWL)
MEDICINE BALL TOSS
YOGA PUSHUPS

PULL
WATER SKIER
PIZZA PAN
CROSS COUNTRY SKIER
ONE ARM ROW
TWO ARM ROW   } PG. 63 - 73
FLIES
SKI POLING
BAR SQUAT PULLUP
BAR ANGLE PULL
BAR JUMP PULLUP

PRESS
MEDICINE BALL TOSS UP
MB SQUAT & TOSS UP
MOUNTAIN CLIMBER
FLOOR JACKS
SIDE TO SIDE PRESS   } PG. 75 - 85
HANDSTAND
PALMS FACING PRESS
PALMS FACE OUT PRESS
PALMS IN PRESS

CURL
123 CRUNCH
REVERSE CRUNCH
BACK EXTENSIONS
SEATED TWIST
SIDE CURLS
MEDICINE BALL LO TO HI
180° +   } PG. 87 - 103
THE "X"
TICK-TOCK
SINGLE LEG STRETCH
SWIMMER
BICYCLE
BALLET EXTENSIONS

TBM
MATRIX I, II, III
SQUAT PRESS
YOGA AIRPLANE   } PG. 105 - 111
BURPEE!
BURPEE EXTRA!

CARDIO
SKIP
JUMP ROPE
STEP UP/DOWN
WALK BRISKLY   } PG. 112
JOG LIGHTLY
JUMPING JACKS

FUNdamental Fitness WORKOUT

WARMUP

YOGA - 3x's PG. 25 - 29

_____ SIT

_____ PUSH

_____ PULL

_____ PRESS

_____ CURL

_____ TBM

_____ CARDIO

YOGA - 3x's PG. 25 - 29

TODAY IS _____

I DID THE CIRCUIT _____ TIMES

IT TOOK ME _____ MINUTES

I FEEL _____!

SIT
WALL SQUAT
MOVING SQUAT
SWISS BALL SQUAT
BACKWARD LUNGE
FORWARD LUNGE
BACK & FORWARD LUNGE
SIT AND LUNGE
SQUAT JUMP
ON YOUR MARK!
} PG. 35 - 47

PUSH
PUSH UP
PUSH UP W/POWER
PLANK
MOVING PLANK
SWISS BALL WALKOUTS
GI JOE (THE CRAWL)
MEDICINE BALL TOSS
YOGA PUSHUPS
} PG. 49 - 61

PULL
WATER SKIER
PIZZA PAN
CROSS COUNTRY SKIER
ONE ARM ROW
TWO ARM ROW
FLIES
SKI POLING
BAR SQUAT PULLUP
BAR ANGLE PULL
BAR JUMP PULLUP
} PG. 63 - 73

PRESS
MEDICINE BALL TOSS UP
MB SQUAT & TOSS UP
MOUNTAIN CLIMBER
FLOOR JACKS
SIDE TO SIDE PRESS
HANDSTAND
PALMS FACING PRESS
PALMS FACE OUT PRESS
PALMS IN PRESS
} PG. 75 - 85

CURL
123 CRUNCH
REVERSE CRUNCH
BACK EXTENSIONS
SEATED TWIST
SIDE CURLS
MEDICINE BALL LO TO HI
180° +
THE "X"
TICK-TOCK
SINGLE LEG STRETCH
SWIMMER
BICYCLE
BALLET EXTENSIONS
} PG. 87 - 103

TBM
MATRIX I, II, III
SQUAT PRESS
YOGA AIRPLANE
BURPEE!
BURPEE EXTRA!
} PG. 105 - 111

CARDIO
SKIP
JUMP ROPE
STEP UP/DOWN
WALK BRISKLY
JOG LIGHTLY
JUMPING JACKS
} PG. 112

FUNdamental Fitness WORKOUT

WARMUP

YOGA - 3x's PG. 25 - 29

_____ SIT

_____ PUSH

_____ PULL

_____ PRESS

_____ CURL

_____ TBM

_____ CARDIO

YOGA - 3x's PG. 25 - 29

TODAY IS _____

I DID THE CIRCUIT _____ TIMES

IT TOOK ME _____ MINUTES

I FEEL _____!

SIT
WALL SQUAT
MOVING SQUAT
SWISS BALL SQUAT
BACKWARD LUNGE
FORWARD LUNGE
BACK & FORWARD LUNGE
SIT AND LUNGE
SQUAT JUMP
ON YOUR MARK!
PG. 35 - 47

PUSH
PUSH UP
PUSH UP W/POWER
PLANK
MOVING PLANK
SWISS BALL WALKOUTS
GI JOE (THE CRAWL)
MEDICINE BALL TOSS
YOGA PUSHUPS
PG. 49 - 61

PULL
WATER SKIER
PIZZA PAN
CROSS COUNTRY SKIER
ONE ARM ROW
TWO ARM ROW
FLIES
SKI POLING
BAR SQUAT PULLUP
BAR ANGLE PULL
BAR JUMP PULLUP
PG. 63 - 73

PRESS
MEDICINE BALL TOSS UP
MB SQUAT & TOSS UP
MOUNTAIN CLIMBER
FLOOR JACKS
SIDE TO SIDE PRESS
HANDSTAND
PALMS FACING PRESS
PALMS FACE OUT PRESS
PALMS IN PRESS
PG. 75 - 85

CURL
123 CRUNCH
REVERSE CRUNCH
BACK EXTENSIONS
SEATED TWIST
SIDE CURLS
MEDICINE BALL LO TO HI
180° +
THE "X"
TICK-TOCK
SINGLE LEG STRETCH
SWIMMER
BICYCLE
BALLET EXTENSIONS
PG. 87 - 103

TBM
MATRIX I, II, III
SQUAT PRESS
YOGA AIRPLANE
BURPEE!
BURPEE EXTRA!
PG. 105 - 111

CARDIO
SKIP
JUMP ROPE
STEP UP/DOWN
WALK BRISKLY
JOG LIGHTLY
JUMPING JACKS
PG. 112

FUNdamental Fitness WORKOUT

WARMUP

YOGA - 3x's PG. 25 - 29

_____ SIT

_____ PUSH

_____ PULL

_____ PRESS

_____ CURL

_____ TBM

_____ CARDIO

YOGA - 3x's PG. 25 - 29

TODAY IS _____

I DID THE CIRCUIT _____ TIMES

IT TOOK ME _____ MINUTES

I FEEL _____!

SIT
WALL SQUAT
MOVING SQUAT
SWISS BALL SQUAT
BACKWARD LUNGE
FORWARD LUNGE
BACK & FORWARD LUNGE
SIT AND LUNGE
SQUAT JUMP
ON YOUR MARK!
} PG. 35 - 47

PUSH
PUSH UP
PUSH UP W/POWER
PLANK
MOVING PLANK
SWISS BALL WALKOUTS
GI JOE (THE CRAWL)
MEDICINE BALL TOSS
YOGA PUSHUPS
} PG. 49 - 61

PULL
WATER SKIER
PIZZA PAN
CROSS COUNTRY SKIER
ONE ARM ROW
TWO ARM ROW
FLIES
SKI POLING
BAR SQUAT PULLUP
BAR ANGLE PULL
BAR JUMP PULLUP
} PG. 63 - 73

PRESS
MEDICINE BALL TOSS UP
MB SQUAT & TOSS UP
MOUNTAIN CLIMBER
FLOOR JACKS
SIDE TO SIDE PRESS
HANDSTAND
PALMS FACING PRESS
PALMS FACE OUT PRESS
PALMS IN PRESS
} PG. 75 - 85

CURL
123 CRUNCH
REVERSE CRUNCH
BACK EXTENSIONS
SEATED TWIST
SIDE CURLS
MEDICINE BALL LO TO HI
$180°$ +
THE "X"
TICK-TOCK
SINGLE LEG STRETCH
SWIMMER
BICYCLE
BALLET EXTENSIONS
} PG. 87 - 103

TBM
MATRIX I, II, III
SQUAT PRESS
YOGA AIRPLANE
BURPEE!
BURPEE EXTRA!
} PG. 105 - 111

CARDIO
SKIP
JUMP ROPE
STEP UP/DOWN
WALK BRISKLY
JOG LIGHTLY
JUMPING JACKS
} PG. 112

FUNdamental Fitness WORKOUT

WARMUP

YOGA - 3x's PG. 25 - 29

_____ SIT

_____ PUSH

_____ PULL

_____ PRESS

_____ CURL

_____ TBM

_____ CARDIO

YOGA - 3x's PG. 25 - 29

TODAY IS _____

I DID THE CIRCUIT _____ TIMES

IT TOOK ME _____ MINUTES

I FEEL _____!

SIT
WALL SQUAT
MOVING SQUAT
SWISS BALL SQUAT
BACKWARD LUNGE
FORWARD LUNGE
BACK & FORWARD LUNGE
SIT AND LUNGE
SQUAT JUMP
ON YOUR MARK!
} PG. 35 - 47

PUSH
PUSH UP
PUSH UP W/POWER
PLANK
MOVING PLANK
SWISS BALL WALKOUTS
GI JOE (THE CRAWL)
MEDICINE BALL TOSS
YOGA PUSHUPS
} PG. 49 - 61

PULL
WATER SKIER
PIZZA PAN
CROSS COUNTRY SKIER
ONE ARM ROW
TWO ARM ROW
FLIES
SKI POLING
BAR SQUAT PULLUP
BAR ANGLE PULL
BAR JUMP PULLUP
} PG. 63 - 73

PRESS
MEDICINE BALL TOSS UP
MB SQUAT & TOSS UP
MOUNTAIN CLIMBER
FLOOR JACKS
SIDE TO SIDE PRESS
HANDSTAND
PALMS FACING PRESS
PALMS FACE OUT PRESS
PALMS IN PRESS
} PG. 75 - 85

CURL
123 CRUNCH
REVERSE CRUNCH
BACK EXTENSIONS
SEATED TWIST
SIDE CURLS
MEDICINE BALL LO TO HI
180° +
THE "X"
TICK-TOCK
SINGLE LEG STRETCH
SWIMMER
BICYCLE
BALLET EXTENSIONS
} PG. 87 - 103

TBM
MATRIX I, II, III
SQUAT PRESS
YOGA AIRPLANE
BURPEE!
BURPEE EXTRA!
} PG. 105 - 111

CARDIO
SKIP
JUMP ROPE
STEP UP/DOWN
WALK BRISKLY
JOG LIGHTLY
JUMPING JACKS
} PG. 112

FUNdamental Fitness WORKOUT

WARMUP

YOGA - 3x's PG. 25 - 29

_____ SIT

_____ PUSH

_____ PULL

_____ PRESS

_____ CURL

_____ TBM

_____ CARDIO

YOGA - 3x's PG. 25 - 29

TODAY IS _____

I DID THE CIRCUIT _____ TIMES

IT TOOK ME _____ MINUTES

I FEEL _____!

SIT
WALL SQUAT
MOVING SQUAT
SWISS BALL SQUAT
BACKWARD LUNGE
FORWARD LUNGE
BACK & FORWARD LUNGE
SIT AND LUNGE
SQUAT JUMP
ON YOUR MARK!
} PG. 35 - 47

PUSH
PUSH UP
PUSH UP W/POWER
PLANK
MOVING PLANK
SWISS BALL WALKOUTS
GI JOE (THE CRAWL)
MEDICINE BALL TOSS
YOGA PUSHUPS
} PG. 49 - 61

PULL
WATER SKIER
PIZZA PAN
CROSS COUNTRY SKIER
ONE ARM ROW
TWO ARM ROW
FLIES
SKI POLING
BAR SQUAT PULLUP
BAR ANGLE PULL
BAR JUMP PULLUP
} PG. 63 - 73

PRESS
MEDICINE BALL TOSS UP
MB SQUAT & TOSS UP
MOUNTAIN CLIMBER
FLOOR JACKS
SIDE TO SIDE PRESS
HANDSTAND
PALMS FACING PRESS
PALMS FACE OUT PRESS
PALMS IN PRESS
} PG. 75 - 85

CURL
123 CRUNCH
REVERSE CRUNCH
BACK EXTENSIONS
SEATED TWIST
SIDE CURLS
MEDICINE BALL LO TO HI
180° +
THE "X"
TICK-TOCK
SINGLE LEG STRETCH
SWIMMER
BICYCLE
BALLET EXTENSIONS
} PG. 87 - 103

TBM
MATRIX I, II, III
SQUAT PRESS
YOGA AIRPLANE
BURPEE!
BURPEE EXTRA!
} PG. 105 - 111

CARDIO
SKIP
JUMP ROPE
STEP UP/DOWN
WALK BRISKLY
JOG LIGHTLY
JUMPING JACKS
} PG. 112

FUNdamental Fitness WORKOUT

WARMUP

YOGA - 3x's PG. 25 - 29

_____ SIT

_____ PUSH

_____ PULL

_____ PRESS

_____ CURL

_____ TBM

_____ CARDIO

YOGA - 3x's PG. 25 - 29

TODAY IS _____

I DID THE CIRCUIT _____ TIMES

IT TOOK ME _____ MINUTES

I FEEL _____!

SIT
WALL SQUAT
MOVING SQUAT
SWISS BALL SQUAT
BACKWARD LUNGE
FORWARD LUNGE
BACK & FORWARD LUNGE
SIT AND LUNGE
SQUAT JUMP
ON YOUR MARK!
} PG. 35 - 47

PUSH
PUSH UP
PUSH UP W/POWER
PLANK
MOVING PLANK
SWISS BALL WALKOUTS
GI JOE (THE CRAWL)
MEDICINE BALL TOSS
YOGA PUSHUPS
} PG. 49 - 61

PULL
WATER SKIER
PIZZA PAN
CROSS COUNTRY SKIER
ONE ARM ROW
TWO ARM ROW
FLIES
SKI POLING
BAR SQUAT PULLUP
BAR ANGLE PULL
BAR JUMP PULLUP
} PG. 63 - 73

PRESS
MEDICINE BALL TOSS UP
MB SQUAT & TOSS UP
MOUNTAIN CLIMBER
FLOOR JACKS
SIDE TO SIDE PRESS
HANDSTAND
PALMS FACING PRESS
PALMS FACE OUT PRESS
PALMS IN PRESS
} PG. 75 - 85

CURL
123 CRUNCH
REVERSE CRUNCH
BACK EXTENSIONS
SEATED TWIST
SIDE CURLS
MEDICINE BALL LO TO HI
180° +
THE "X"
TICK-TOCK
SINGLE LEG STRETCH
SWIMMER
BICYCLE
BALLET EXTENSIONS
} PG. 87 - 103

TBM
MATRIX I, II, III
SQUAT PRESS
YOGA AIRPLANE
BURPEE!
BURPEE EXTRA!
} PG. 105 - 111

CARDIO
SKIP
JUMP ROPE
STEP UP/DOWN
WALK BRISKLY
JOG LIGHTLY
JUMPING JACKS
} PG. 112

FUNdamental Fitness WORKOUT

WARMUP

YOGA - 3x's PG. 25 - 29

_____ SIT

_____ PUSH

_____ PULL

_____ PRESS

_____ CURL

_____ TBM

_____ CARDIO

YOGA - 3x's PG. 25 - 29

TODAY IS _____

I DID THE CIRCUIT _____ TIMES

IT TOOK ME _____ MINUTES

I FEEL _____!

SIT
WALL SQUAT
MOVING SQUAT
SWISS BALL SQUAT
BACKWARD LUNGE
FORWARD LUNGE
BACK & FORWARD LUNGE
SIT AND LUNGE
SQUAT JUMP
ON YOUR MARK!
} PG. 35 - 47

PUSH
PUSH UP
PUSH UP W/POWER
PLANK
MOVING PLANK
SWISS BALL WALKOUTS
GI JOE (THE CRAWL)
MEDICINE BALL TOSS
YOGA PUSHUPS
} PG. 49 - 61

PULL
WATER SKIER
PIZZA PAN
CROSS COUNTRY SKIER
ONE ARM ROW
TWO ARM ROW
FLIES
SKI POLING
BAR SQUAT PULLUP
BAR ANGLE PULL
BAR JUMP PULLUP
} PG. 63 - 73

PRESS
MEDICINE BALL TOSS UP
MB SQUAT & TOSS UP
MOUNTAIN CLIMBER
FLOOR JACKS
SIDE TO SIDE PRESS
HANDSTAND
PALMS FACING PRESS
PALMS FACE OUT PRESS
PALMS IN PRESS
} PG. 75 - 85

CURL
123 CRUNCH
REVERSE CRUNCH
BACK EXTENSIONS
SEATED TWIST
SIDE CURLS
MEDICINE BALL LO TO HI
180° +
THE "X"
TICK-TOCK
SINGLE LEG STRETCH
SWIMMER
BICYCLE
BALLET EXTENSIONS
} PG. 87 - 103

TBM
MATRIX I, II, III
SQUAT PRESS
YOGA AIRPLANE
BURPEE!
BURPEE EXTRA!
} PG. 105 - 111

CARDIO
SKIP
JUMP ROPE
STEP UP/DOWN
WALK BRISKLY
JOG LIGHTLY
JUMPING JACKS
} PG. 112

FUNdamental Fitness WORKOUT

WARMUP

YOGA - 3x's PG. 25 - 29

_____ SIT

_____ PUSH

_____ PULL

_____ PRESS

_____ CURL

_____ TBM

_____ CARDIO

YOGA - 3x's PG. 25 - 29

TODAY IS _____

I DID THE CIRCUIT _____ TIMES

IT TOOK ME _____ MINUTES

I FEEL _____!

SIT
WALL SQUAT
MOVING SQUAT
SWISS BALL SQUAT
BACKWARD LUNGE
FORWARD LUNGE
BACK & FORWARD LUNGE
SIT AND LUNGE
SQUAT JUMP
ON YOUR MARK!
} PG. 35 - 47

PUSH
PUSH UP
PUSH UP W/POWER
PLANK
MOVING PLANK
SWISS BALL WALKOUTS
GI JOE (THE CRAWL)
MEDICINE BALL TOSS
YOGA PUSHUPS
} PG. 49 - 61

PULL
WATER SKIER
PIZZA PAN
CROSS COUNTRY SKIER
ONE ARM ROW
TWO ARM ROW
FLIES
SKI POLING
BAR SQUAT PULLUP
BAR ANGLE PULL
BAR JUMP PULLUP
} PG. 63 - 73

PRESS
MEDICINE BALL TOSS UP
MB SQUAT & TOSS UP
MOUNTAIN CLIMBER
FLOOR JACKS
SIDE TO SIDE PRESS
HANDSTAND
PALMS FACING PRESS
PALMS FACE OUT PRESS
PALMS IN PRESS
} PG. 75 - 85

CURL
123 CRUNCH
REVERSE CRUNCH
BACK EXTENSIONS
SEATED TWIST
SIDE CURLS
MEDICINE BALL LO TO HI
180° +
THE "X"
TICK-TOCK
SINGLE LEG STRETCH
SWIMMER
BICYCLE
BALLET EXTENSIONS
} PG. 87 - 103

TBM
MATRIX I, II, III
SQUAT PRESS
YOGA AIRPLANE
BURPEE!
BURPEE EXTRA!
} PG. 105 - 111

CARDIO
SKIP
JUMP ROPE
STEP UP/DOWN
WALK BRISKLY
JOG LIGHTLY
JUMPING JACKS
} PG. 112

FUNdamental Fitness WORKOUT

WARMUP

YOGA - 3x's PG. 25 - 29

_____ SIT

_____ PUSH

_____ PULL

_____ PRESS

_____ CURL

_____ TBM

_____ CARDIO

YOGA - 3x's PG. 25 - 29

TODAY IS _____

I DID THE CIRCUIT _____ TIMES

IT TOOK ME _____ MINUTES

I FEEL _____!

SIT
WALL SQUAT
MOVING SQUAT
SWISS BALL SQUAT
BACKWARD LUNGE
FORWARD LUNGE
BACK & FORWARD LUNGE
SIT AND LUNGE
SQUAT JUMP
ON YOUR MARK!
} PG. 35 - 47

PUSH
PUSH UP
PUSH UP W/POWER
PLANK
MOVING PLANK
SWISS BALL WALKOUTS
GI JOE (THE CRAWL)
MEDICINE BALL TOSS
YOGA PUSHUPS
} PG. 49 - 61

PULL
WATER SKIER
PIZZA PAN
CROSS COUNTRY SKIER
ONE ARM ROW
TWO ARM ROW
FLIES
SKI POLING
BAR SQUAT PULLUP
BAR ANGLE PULL
BAR JUMP PULLUP
} PG. 63 - 73

PRESS
MEDICINE BALL TOSS UP
MB SQUAT & TOSS UP
MOUNTAIN CLIMBER
FLOOR JACKS
SIDE TO SIDE PRESS
HANDSTAND
PALMS FACING PRESS
PALMS FACE OUT PRESS
PALMS IN PRESS
} PG. 75 - 85

CURL
123 CRUNCH
REVERSE CRUNCH
BACK EXTENSIONS
SEATED TWIST
SIDE CURLS
MEDICINE BALL LO TO HI
$180°$ +
THE "X"
TICK-TOCK
SINGLE LEG STRETCH
SWIMMER
BICYCLE
BALLET EXTENSIONS
} PG. 87 - 103

TBM
MATRIX I, II, III
SQUAT PRESS
YOGA AIRPLANE
BURPEE!
BURPEE EXTRA!
} PG. 105 - 111

CARDIO
SKIP
JUMP ROPE
STEP UP/DOWN
WALK BRISKLY
JOG LIGHTLY
JUMPING JACKS
} PG. 112

FUNdamental Fitness WORKOUT

WARMUP

YOGA - 3x's PG. 25 - 29

_____ SIT

_____ PUSH

_____ PULL

_____ PRESS

_____ CURL

_____ TBM

_____ CARDIO

YOGA - 3x's PG. 25 - 29

TODAY IS _____

I DID THE CIRCUIT _____ TIMES

IT TOOK ME _____ MINUTES

I FEEL _____!

SIT
WALL SQUAT
MOVING SQUAT
SWISS BALL SQUAT
BACKWARD LUNGE
FORWARD LUNGE
BACK & FORWARD LUNGE
SIT AND LUNGE
SQUAT JUMP
ON YOUR MARK!
} PG. 35 - 47

PUSH
PUSH UP
PUSH UP W/POWER
PLANK
MOVING PLANK
SWISS BALL WALKOUTS
GI JOE (THE CRAWL)
MEDICINE BALL TOSS
YOGA PUSHUPS
} PG. 49 - 61

PULL
WATER SKIER
PIZZA PAN
CROSS COUNTRY SKIER
ONE ARM ROW
TWO ARM ROW
FLIES
SKI POLING
BAR SQUAT PULLUP
BAR ANGLE PULL
BAR JUMP PULLUP
} PG. 63 - 73

PRESS
MEDICINE BALL TOSS UP
MB SQUAT & TOSS UP
MOUNTAIN CLIMBER
FLOOR JACKS
SIDE TO SIDE PRESS
HANDSTAND
PALMS FACING PRESS
PALMS FACE OUT PRESS
PALMS IN PRESS
} PG. 75 - 85

CURL
123 CRUNCH
REVERSE CRUNCH
BACK EXTENSIONS
SEATED TWIST
SIDE CURLS
MEDICINE BALL LO TO HI
180° +
THE "X"
TICK-TOCK
SINGLE LEG STRETCH
SWIMMER
BICYCLE
BALLET EXTENSIONS
} PG. 87 - 103

TBM
MATRIX I, II, III
SQUAT PRESS
YOGA AIRPLANE
BURPEE!
BURPEE EXTRA!
} PG. 105 - 111

CARDIO
SKIP
JUMP ROPE
STEP UP/DOWN
WALK BRISKLY
JOG LIGHTLY
JUMPING JACKS
} PG. 112

FUNdamental Fitness WORKOUT

WARMUP

YOGA - 3x's PG. 25 - 29

_____ SIT

_____ PUSH

_____ PULL

_____ PRESS

_____ CURL

_____ TBM

_____ CARDIO

YOGA - 3x's PG. 25 - 29

TODAY IS _____

I DID THE CIRCUIT _____ TIMES

IT TOOK ME _____ MINUTES

I FEEL _____!

SIT
WALL SQUAT
MOVING SQUAT
SWISS BALL SQUAT
BACKWARD LUNGE
FORWARD LUNGE
BACK & FORWARD LUNGE
SIT AND LUNGE
SQUAT JUMP
ON YOUR MARK!
} PG. 35 - 47

PUSH
PUSH UP
PUSH UP W/POWER
PLANK
MOVING PLANK
SWISS BALL WALKOUTS
GI JOE (THE CRAWL)
MEDICINE BALL TOSS
YOGA PUSHUPS
} PG. 49 - 61

PULL
WATER SKIER
PIZZA PAN
CROSS COUNTRY SKIER
ONE ARM ROW
TWO ARM ROW
FLIES
SKI POLING
BAR SQUAT PULLUP
BAR ANGLE PULL
BAR JUMP PULLUP
} PG. 63 - 73

PRESS
MEDICINE BALL TOSS UP
MB SQUAT & TOSS UP
MOUNTAIN CLIMBER
FLOOR JACKS
SIDE TO SIDE PRESS
HANDSTAND
PALMS FACING PRESS
PALMS FACE OUT PRESS
PALMS IN PRESS
} PG. 75 - 85

CURL
123 CRUNCH
REVERSE CRUNCH
BACK EXTENSIONS
SEATED TWIST
SIDE CURLS
MEDICINE BALL LO TO HI
180° +
THE "X"
TICK-TOCK
SINGLE LEG STRETCH
SWIMMER
BICYCLE
BALLET EXTENSIONS
} PG. 87 - 103

TBM
MATRIX I, II, III
SQUAT PRESS
YOGA AIRPLANE
BURPEE!
BURPEE EXTRA!
} PG. 105 - 111

CARDIO
SKIP
JUMP ROPE
STEP UP/DOWN
WALK BRISKLY
JOG LIGHTLY
JUMPING JACKS
} PG. 112

FUNdamental Fitness WORKOUT

WARMUP

YOGA - 3x's PG. 25 - 29

_____ SIT

_____ PUSH

_____ PULL

_____ PRESS

_____ CURL

_____ TBM

_____ CARDIO

YOGA - 3x's PG. 25 - 29

TODAY IS _____

I DID THE CIRCUIT _____ TIMES

IT TOOK ME _____ MINUTES

I FEEL _____!

SIT
WALL SQUAT
MOVING SQUAT
SWISS BALL SQUAT
BACKWARD LUNGE
FORWARD LUNGE
BACK & FORWARD LUNGE
SIT AND LUNGE
SQUAT JUMP
ON YOUR MARK!
} PG. 35 - 47

PUSH
PUSH UP
PUSH UP W/POWER
PLANK
MOVING PLANK
SWISS BALL WALKOUTS
GI JOE (THE CRAWL)
MEDICINE BALL TOSS
YOGA PUSHUPS
} PG. 49 - 61

PULL
WATER SKIER
PIZZA PAN
CROSS COUNTRY SKIER
ONE ARM ROW
TWO ARM ROW
FLIES
SKI POLING
BAR SQUAT PULLUP
BAR ANGLE PULL
BAR JUMP PULLUP
} PG. 63 - 73

PRESS
MEDICINE BALL TOSS UP
MB SQUAT & TOSS UP
MOUNTAIN CLIMBER
FLOOR JACKS
SIDE TO SIDE PRESS
HANDSTAND
PALMS FACING PRESS
PALMS FACE OUT PRESS
PALMS IN PRESS
} PG. 75 - 85

CURL
123 CRUNCH
REVERSE CRUNCH
BACK EXTENSIONS
SEATED TWIST
SIDE CURLS
MEDICINE BALL LO TO HI
180° +
THE "X"
TICK-TOCK
SINGLE LEG STRETCH
SWIMMER
BICYCLE
BALLET EXTENSIONS
} PG. 87 - 103

TBM
MATRIX I, II, III
SQUAT PRESS
YOGA AIRPLANE
BURPEE!
BURPEE EXTRA!
} PG. 105 - 111

CARDIO
SKIP
JUMP ROPE
STEP UP/DOWN
WALK BRISKLY
JOG LIGHTLY
JUMPING JACKS
} PG. 112

FUNdamental Fitness WORKOUT

WARMUP

YOGA - 3x's PG. 25 - 29

_____ SIT

_____ PUSH

_____ PULL

_____ PRESS

_____ CURL

_____ TBM

_____ CARDIO

YOGA - 3x's PG. 25 - 29

TODAY IS _____

I DID THE CIRCUIT _____ TIMES

IT TOOK ME _____ MINUTES

I FEEL _____!

SIT
WALL SQUAT
MOVING SQUAT
SWISS BALL SQUAT
BACKWARD LUNGE
FORWARD LUNGE
BACK & FORWARD LUNGE
SIT AND LUNGE
SQUAT JUMP
ON YOUR MARK!
} PG. 35 - 47

PUSH
PUSH UP
PUSH UP W/POWER
PLANK
MOVING PLANK
SWISS BALL WALKOUTS
GI JOE (THE CRAWL)
MEDICINE BALL TOSS
YOGA PUSHUPS
} PG. 49 - 61

PULL
WATER SKIER
PIZZA PAN
CROSS COUNTRY SKIER
ONE ARM ROW
TWO ARM ROW
FLIES
SKI POLING
BAR SQUAT PULLUP
BAR ANGLE PULL
BAR JUMP PULLUP
} PG. 63 - 73

PRESS
MEDICINE BALL TOSS UP
MB SQUAT & TOSS UP
MOUNTAIN CLIMBER
FLOOR JACKS
SIDE TO SIDE PRESS
HANDSTAND
PALMS FACING PRESS
PALMS FACE OUT PRESS
PALMS IN PRESS
} PG. 75 - 85

CURL
123 CRUNCH
REVERSE CRUNCH
BACK EXTENSIONS
SEATED TWIST
SIDE CURLS
MEDICINE BALL LO TO HI
$180°$ +
THE "X"
TICK-TOCK
SINGLE LEG STRETCH
SWIMMER
BICYCLE
BALLET EXTENSIONS
} PG. 87 - 103

TBM
MATRIX I, II, III
SQUAT PRESS
YOGA AIRPLANE
BURPEE!
BURPEE EXTRA!
} PG. 105 - 111

CARDIO
SKIP
JUMP ROPE
STEP UP/DOWN
WALK BRISKLY
JOG LIGHTLY
JUMPING JACKS
} PG. 112

FUNdamental Fitness WORKOUT

WARMUP

YOGA - 3x's PG. 25 - 29

_____ SIT

_____ PUSH

_____ PULL

_____ PRESS

_____ CURL

_____ TBM

_____ CARDIO

YOGA - 3x's PG. 25 - 29

TODAY IS _____

I DID THE CIRCUIT _____ TIMES

IT TOOK ME _____ MINUTES

I FEEL _____!

SIT
WALL SQUAT
MOVING SQUAT
SWISS BALL SQUAT
BACKWARD LUNGE
FORWARD LUNGE
BACK & FORWARD LUNGE
SIT AND LUNGE
SQUAT JUMP
ON YOUR MARK!
} PG. 35 - 47

PUSH
PUSH UP
PUSH UP W/POWER
PLANK
MOVING PLANK
SWISS BALL WALKOUTS
GI JOE (THE CRAWL)
MEDICINE BALL TOSS
YOGA PUSHUPS
} PG. 49 - 61

PULL
WATER SKIER
PIZZA PAN
CROSS COUNTRY SKIER
ONE ARM ROW
TWO ARM ROW
FLIES
SKI POLING
BAR SQUAT PULLUP
BAR ANGLE PULL
BAR JUMP PULLUP
} PG. 63 - 73

PRESS
MEDICINE BALL TOSS UP
MB SQUAT & TOSS UP
MOUNTAIN CLIMBER
FLOOR JACKS
SIDE TO SIDE PRESS
HANDSTAND
PALMS FACING PRESS
PALMS FACE OUT PRESS
PALMS IN PRESS
} PG. 75 - 85

CURL
123 CRUNCH
REVERSE CRUNCH
BACK EXTENSIONS
SEATED TWIST
SIDE CURLS
MEDICINE BALL LO TO HI
180° +
THE "X"
TICK-TOCK
SINGLE LEG STRETCH
SWIMMER
BICYCLE
BALLET EXTENSIONS
} PG. 87 - 103

TBM
MATRIX I, II, III
SQUAT PRESS
YOGA AIRPLANE
BURPEE!
BURPEE EXTRA!
} PG. 105 - 111

CARDIO
SKIP
JUMP ROPE
STEP UP/DOWN
WALK BRISKLY
JOG LIGHTLY
JUMPING JACKS
} PG. 112

FUNdamental Fitness WORKOUT

WARMUP

YOGA - 3x's PG. 25 - 29

_____ SIT

_____ PUSH

_____ PULL

_____ PRESS

_____ CURL

_____ TBM

_____ CARDIO

YOGA - 3x's PG. 25 - 29

TODAY IS _____

I DID THE CIRCUIT _____ TIMES

IT TOOK ME _____ MINUTES

I FEEL _____!

SIT
WALL SQUAT
MOVING SQUAT
SWISS BALL SQUAT
BACKWARD LUNGE
FORWARD LUNGE
BACK & FORWARD LUNGE
SIT AND LUNGE
SQUAT JUMP
ON YOUR MARK!
} PG. 35 - 47

PUSH
PUSH UP
PUSH UP W/POWER
PLANK
MOVING PLANK
SWISS BALL WALKOUTS
GI JOE (THE CRAWL)
MEDICINE BALL TOSS
YOGA PUSHUPS
} PG. 49 - 61

PULL
WATER SKIER
PIZZA PAN
CROSS COUNTRY SKIER
ONE ARM ROW
TWO ARM ROW
FLIES
SKI POLING
BAR SQUAT PULLUP
BAR ANGLE PULL
BAR JUMP PULLUP
} PG. 63 - 73

PRESS
MEDICINE BALL TOSS UP
MB SQUAT & TOSS UP
MOUNTAIN CLIMBER
FLOOR JACKS
SIDE TO SIDE PRESS
HANDSTAND
PALMS FACING PRESS
PALMS FACE OUT PRESS
PALMS IN PRESS
} PG. 75 - 85

CURL
123 CRUNCH
REVERSE CRUNCH
BACK EXTENSIONS
SEATED TWIST
SIDE CURLS
MEDICINE BALL LO TO HI
180° +
THE "X"
TICK-TOCK
SINGLE LEG STRETCH
SWIMMER
BICYCLE
BALLET EXTENSIONS
} PG. 87 - 103

TBM
MATRIX I, II, III
SQUAT PRESS
YOGA AIRPLANE
BURPEE!
BURPEE EXTRA!
} PG. 105 - 111

CARDIO
SKIP
JUMP ROPE
STEP UP/DOWN
WALK BRISKLY
JOG LIGHTLY
JUMPING JACKS
} PG. 112

FUNdamental Fitness WORKOUT

WARMUP

YOGA - 3x's PG. 25 - 29

_____ SIT

_____ PUSH

_____ PULL

_____ PRESS

_____ CURL

_____ TBM

_____ CARDIO

YOGA - 3x's PG. 25 - 29

TODAY IS _____

I DID THE CIRCUIT _____ TIMES

IT TOOK ME _____ MINUTES

I FEEL _____!

SIT
WALL SQUAT
MOVING SQUAT
SWISS BALL SQUAT
BACKWARD LUNGE
FORWARD LUNGE
BACK & FORWARD LUNGE
SIT AND LUNGE
SQUAT JUMP
ON YOUR MARK!
} PG. 35 - 47

PUSH
PUSH UP
PUSH UP W/POWER
PLANK
MOVING PLANK
SWISS BALL WALKOUTS
GI JOE (THE CRAWL)
MEDICINE BALL TOSS
YOGA PUSHUPS
} PG. 49 - 61

PULL
WATER SKIER
PIZZA PAN
CROSS COUNTRY SKIER
ONE ARM ROW
TWO ARM ROW
FLIES
SKI POLING
BAR SQUAT PULLUP
BAR ANGLE PULL
BAR JUMP PULLUP
} PG. 63 - 73

PRESS
MEDICINE BALL TOSS UP
MB SQUAT & TOSS UP
MOUNTAIN CLIMBER
FLOOR JACKS
SIDE TO SIDE PRESS
HANDSTAND
PALMS FACING PRESS
PALMS FACE OUT PRESS
PALMS IN PRESS
} PG. 75 - 85

CURL
123 CRUNCH
REVERSE CRUNCH
BACK EXTENSIONS
SEATED TWIST
SIDE CURLS
MEDICINE BALL LO TO HI
180° +
THE "X"
TICK-TOCK
SINGLE LEG STRETCH
SWIMMER
BICYCLE
BALLET EXTENSIONS
} PG. 87 - 103

TBM
MATRIX I, II, III
SQUAT PRESS
YOGA AIRPLANE
BURPEE!
BURPEE EXTRA!
} PG. 105 - 111

CARDIO
SKIP
JUMP ROPE
STEP UP/DOWN
WALK BRISKLY
JOG LIGHTLY
JUMPING JACKS
} PG. 112

✻ ✻

ABOUT THE AUTHOR

Jen Hoeft is an ACE certified personal trainer, a JohnnyG certified spin instructor, and a 19-year veteran of group fitness training. As a professional drummer, she has combined her passion for music and wellness into a unique and real approach to knowing, challenging, and celebrating the body inside and out. As a women's fitness expert, Jen is a health consultant and writer for *Modern Drummer* magazine, and the host of the *Fit in the Fast Lane* series of fitness tips for travelers. Jen studies martial arts and is an avid swimmer and cyclist.

✻ ✻ ✻ ✻ ✻ ✻ ✻ ✻ ✻ ✻ ✻ ✻ ✻ ✻ ✻ ✻ ✻ ✻